RAISING KIDS

It Ain't Easy, but It Can Be Fun

Stan Kary

VANTAGE PRESS

New York

FIRST EDITION

Copyright © 1992 by Stan Kary

Published by Vantage Press, Inc.
516 West 34th Street, New York, New York 10001

Manufactured in the United States of America

ISBN: 0-533-09576-X

Library of Congress Catalog Card No.: 91-90891

0 9 8 7 6 5 4

To
Andrew Kary and
Mary Kary,
my grandparents,
who always made 4th Street seem like heaven

Contents

Preface   vii
Acknowledgments   ix

1. The Overall Plan..   1
2. Pavlov's Dogs or How I Learned
   to Be Afraid...   5
3. Learning—Learning—Learning or Isn't My
   Little Girl Cute?..   12
4. How It All Gets Started   22
5. How to Punish Effectively...........................   28
6. Making Things Easy...................................   47
7. Let's Change the Behavior   57
8. Schedules of Reinforcement and Finding
   Rewards That Work   77
9. Let's Talk about Sex   86
10. Learning How to Share Love   95
11. Blended Family or
    Are All These Kids Ours?...........................   109
12. How to Handle Stress   123

Preface

This book is based on many years of psychological research. Many psychologists and researchers before me have laid down the principles that are used in this book. Many of these principles are common knowledge and can be found in numerous texts, while others are a bit more obscure. In one sense, I have added little but my own experience, while on the other hand, I have tried to make much of the psychological research available to the average reader in a form that they may find easy to read and applicable to their life.

If I have interested you in the field of psychology I would recommend a course in psychology at the college level. If I have teased your curiosity about psychology and its application to everyday life, there are many books available to satisfy your curiosity. If you have had no experience in psychology at all I would recommend a good introductory psychology text.

Acknowledgments

I would like to thank Carol Kruchowski for her careful reading of the original manuscript. As a parent she was able to offer helpful comments. To Jim Caldwell, whose years of grade school teaching were a valuable source of information. To Dr. Gerald Schaeffer, a practicing psychologist, who kept me in line with psychological principles. To Dick Teneau, who offered many tips in writing and style of presentation. To Dr. Charles Rock, who also aided with psychological comments and style of presentation. To Joe Lupo, whose command of the English language is second to none. To Dr. Linda Wickstra, who helped in putting together the final form of this brief book. To Walter and Pam Clark, Eric and Barb Nelson, and John and Cathy Vencill the "Saturday Night Bridge Club" that helped me find a name for this work somewhere between one no-trump and four hearts. To all of my children: Merianna, John, Nancy, Amanda, Matthew, and Ryan, whose love and behavior guided me to becoming a parent.

Finally, Cindy my wife, who was always patient and stopped to help, no matter what she was doing. Without her love and support I could have never written this book, nor understood the real job of becoming a parent.

Clearly, if any of you reading this have been helped to become a better parent we owe it to the above cast, and any shortcomings are my own.

All graphs by Charles Rock and Dick Teneau
Photographic work by Len Kroesen.

RAISING KIDS

1. The Overall Plan

Does this sound like your child? You tell him something a hundred times and it seems to go in one ear and out the other. Your daughter doesn't seem to clean up her room and you wonder which pigpen she wandered in from. Your children just want to sit around and watch television and the only way you can get them to do something is to do every step of the task with them. Or you go somewhere and your child throws such a fit you are about ready to sell him at the next K-Mart blue light special.

Now, there have been many books written about "how to raise kids." So you're probably wondering why another one? Well, this one really is different. It is different because, along with trying to help you raise your children and turn around the examples you've just read, I look at the outcomes of such discipline and training. I also attempt to offer you a general philosophy about raising children. I want to share some of my experiences, not because I've been the world's greatest parent, not because I have all of the answers, but because I care about rearing children and seriously believe my triumphs and, yes, my failures may be helpful to you. Think of the information in this book as a curriculum for your children. Remember YOU are the most important educator your children will ever have, and YOU have the most powerful influence on their lives.

Another reason this book is different is that right up front I make certain basic assumptions, with which few parents disagree and which are based on scientific data. After all, if we are going to raise children, we should educate them in the best manner possible and in a way that leads to their becoming healthy, loving adults. Otherwise, why bother with the whole rearing process?

In the course of this book I make a number of assumptions about training outcomes, but it should be clear that we train children not just so they will behave correctly today . . . but so that their behavior will have specific positive results in the future. This is precisely where other child-rearing books have left parents short. They tell you as a parent what you should do with little "Johnny or Sally" now, but most of the time they don't discuss what your training will lead to in the future. They don't warn you about the consequences of today's training.

Now, it isn't all that hard. God gave Moses Ten Commandments and, following that time-honored tradition, you too have only ten things that you will have the children doing. It is an important ten points, and with these as a foundation, who knows what you may accomplish? Think of it as an insurance policy for all of your training as well as an insurance policy for maintaining our culture. When our job as parents and teachers is complete, we want the child to:

1. Be self-sufficient and be able to live on his or her own.
2. Be able to respect authority and follow the rules of our society or culture, not blindly but when appropriate.
3. Be a good mother or father to his or her children.
4. Be able to handle his or her own finances in a responsible manner. That is to pay the bills on

time and not to buy things that they cannot afford.

5. Be concerned about his or her immediate environment as well as the greater world within which he or she lives.
6. Not steal or lie.
7. Not take another life.
8. Treat all people with respect and treat all people the same way he or she wants to be treated.
9. Love and be loved in return.
10. Say NO to drugs!

Now, that's not so bad, is it? Just think, after reading this book you will be on the road to accomplishing these goals with your children. Remember, the job of raising our children is to eventually work ourselves out of the job. That doesn't mean that we want to end our relationship with our children, but at some point we must give up the task. After all, we won't live forever, and if the kids aren't independent and self-sufficient at some point, how can we pass on our culture to them? Again, it doesn't mean that we don't love them, but how will they eat or take care of our grandchildren if at some time our job as a parent isn't finished?

Here is another way of looking at it. Never before have children held so much power in their hands. Our children not only will control their own immediate destiny, but they will control the very survival of the earth as we have known it. The learning that we put in their heads is what they will carry to adulthood with them, and it is these learned values by which they will make their decisions. As a parent, I should like the world to be without war, poverty, or prejudice. I should like all of our children's, children's . . . children to live in a world of peace and love such as the world has never known. We today hold the potential of giving them that world and it starts as simply as loving and spending time with our children as they grow up today.

I am convinced that this book can help you achieve these ten goals. Even if we should fall a bit short, look at what we will have accomplished, and what have you got to lose?

There is one final thing I ask of you in this chapter. Please read this book as you would a novel. Start with chapter 1 (if you are reading this, you are obviously in the right place) and read the chapters in consecutive order. This book is not intended to be just an encyclopedia or cookbook for problem children. Although there are numerous examples, this book is designed to give you an overall view and a new philosophy about raising children. As a result, when problems arise, as they surely will, you will not need to run to some cookbook for problems. After you have completed this book, you will have an overall plan that will enable you to handle problems as they arise.

No book can answer every single question or problem about raising children. But because of your overall plan, you will have agreed upon goals that are important to you as a parent so that when problems arise, you can ask yourself, "How does this fit into my plan?" Also, some problems are beyond the scope of this book and seeking out a mental health professional for an evaluation or some extra help is sometimes necessary.

Good luck and let's get started.

2. Pavlov's Dogs or How I Learned to Be Afraid

The next three chapters aren't going to be the easiest you have ever read. Now, they aren't that hard, but the concepts covered will help you understand the rest of the book. Be a little patient as you read these first chapters. It can help you be a better parent, and you may even begin to enjoy being a parent. No text is ever going to make all of child-rearing fun. Sometimes it is no fun at all! But overall it is a delightful experience, and it is easily the most important job you will do in your entire life. I know that you want to do it right, and I think this book can help you.

We begin by looking at dogs. It doesn't mean that we are dogs or that our children are animals (although some parents wonder), but human behavior is very complex and using animals allows us to observe certain learning concepts in a much simpler form. Later, I apply these principles to the development of emotions in children. With this approach you can begin to understand some of the psychological development of children, but for now, let's deal with dogs.

In the early 1900's a Russian physiologist and Nobel Prize winner, Ivan Petrovich Pavlov, developed what we today call classical conditioning. Basically, he rang a bell and shortly after (about one-half to five seconds later) he gave food to the dog. After about twelve to twenty of these trials, the dog began to salivate at the sound of the bell. It is as if the bell became a signal to the dog that food was on the way. This set of operations, ringing the bell followed by the administration of food, is often referred to as the basic classical conditioning set of operations or paradigm. Almost all of this chapter is based on some aspect of this basic paradigm.

After the dog salivates to the sound of the bell, the response of salivation will be given to other stimuli (things) that are similar to the original conditioning stimulus, in our example, the bell. This is called stimulus generalization. As an example, instead of using a bell, let's teach the animal to salivate to a tone, like middle C on the piano. We plunk the key, the note is sounded, and we give the dog food. After several trials, we press the key and, like magic, the dog begins to salivate without being given any food. But what would happen if we presented the dog with another tone that was close to the original tone? Would the dog still salivate? Well, if the tone is close enough to our original tone, yes, the dog will salivate. The salivation or response that we get from the animal may not be as great as the original response (we wouldn't get quite as much saliva), but we would still get a significant or strong response. When the dog responds by salivating, it is generalizing the response of salivation to a like or similar stimulus. Hence, the term *stimulus generalization*. In order for this to work, the stimulus must be almost like the original stimulus. If it is not (e.g., the sound of a drum or any other different sound), the dog will not respond.

In a slightly different form, the idea of generalization is an old one for everyone. Remember when you were in school or when you went shopping at a local shopping mall and saw someone in the distance. She was about the same height and weight as a friend of yours. She had on the exact same coat that a friend of yours wears. You took a second look to see if it really was your friend. If it wasn't your friend, your case of mistaken identity was really stimulus generalization. There were enough "similar" stimuli or "things" present to remind you of a friend of yours and you took that second look just to be sure. We see later that the looking was really a behavior that belongs to another form of learning, namely, operant conditioning. For now, however, the point is that we, and the dog, will respond in some manner if the new stimulus is close enough to the original stimulus.

Of the many concepts in classical conditioning, one final concept to look at is extinction. What would happen if we kept ringing the bell but stopped giving the food? Will the dog keep salivating? No! Like a fireman extinguishing a fire with his hose, the bell, now followed by nothing, will extinguish or eliminate the salivation. It is as if the dog were saying to himself, "Why salivate? There isn't any food coming." When classical conditioning takes place it is not merely the fact that the stimulus is present, close in time and space (contiguity) . . . the stimulus also brings with it some information. In our first example, the bell indicated that food was coming. When the bell or tone is no longer followed by food, the informational component is lost and the response extinguishes. We will need this idea later, so just tuck it away for now.

If you have been reading this far, you are probably wondering what this has to do with raising and disciplining children. One more example and it will start to become crystal clear.

In 1920, John B. Watson and Rosalie Rayner published an experiment about a small child they called Albert. When Albert was eleven months old they showed him a white rat, and a few seconds later, one of the researchers standing behind the boy hit a steel pipe with a hammer. As you might suspect, this startled the child, and after a few repeats of the white rat and the "BANG," the child became afraid of the white rat and cried. From then on, every time they showed a white rat to Albert, he cried and showed a marked fear of the white furry creature. He also showed fear when he was exposed to other white furrylike things (remember stimulus generalization), such as a rabbit.

Another important point to this experiment is human emotions. Whenever we are in the presence of some stimulus or stimulus situation, we attach some emotions to that thing. When we are confronted with that situation or thing again, it elicits the same emotion that has been learned or associated with it.

A few examples will help clear things up. Most psychologists try to tell expectant mothers about the benefits of breast-feeding from a nutritional point of view. But consider breast-feeding from the psychological viewpoint. A small child is being held and is being breast-fed. What kind of emotion do you think the child is experiencing? A very positive or pleasant one. What things are present while the child is nursing? There certainly is the mother, her physical contact, and usually her voice. Yes, her voice. When my children were young and my wife nursed them she would often sing or talk to them. In the process of nursing the mother's body contact with the child and her soothing voice became associated with the positive emotion the child was experiencing. It may come as a surprise, but we aren't born with likes, dislikes, or fears. What we are born with is the *potential to learn* to like, dislike, or fear things in the curious world in which we live. Thus we make both fearful, positive, or pleasant emotional attachments after birth, by means of classical conditioning.

Think of the child who is bottle-fed and isn't usually held while being fed. Think of this child after he's a little older. All the potentially positive things that could be learned are being missed, totally. In today's busy world with both parents working, think of the emotional vacuum that too many kids start life with. And, as the children grow, what emotional foundation do they have to build on? In too many cases, little if any. Now, don't be concerned. If your child wasn't breast-fed, he or she will still be perfectly normal. Obviously, the emotional bonding you make with your child can be obtained in a number of ways. I was just using breast-feeding as an easy example to make my point concerning emotional attachments.

In the process of growing up, children experience a wide range of events that are filled with strong emotions which may have a positive as well as a negative effect upon their emotional development.

A child is hit with a belt or he is playing hide-and-seek and accidentally gets locked into a closet. Later when the same child walks by the belt hanging on the hook, or tries to go to sleep in his room alone and in the dark—bingo—he's scared to death. And we know why.

Another example. Picture a small white child playing in the sandbox in some public park with a small black child (or an Oriental child or a child of Spanish origin or a Jewish child or any child who is somewhat different from the first child). Along comes his mother, who, for the sake of our example, doesn't like people who are different from her. She sees her child and scolds or even spanks her child for playing with the "different" child. It doesn't take an Einstein to figure out what emotion the white child will feel in the presence of the "different" child. An unpleasant emotion or fear is attached to the stimulus of the mother's wrath. So when the little child sees another "different" child, the emotion of fear is elicited. How many examples of this type of behavior have parents exhibited in relation to blacks, whites, Chicanos, Orientals, Poles, Catholics, and so on, and at what price in terms of the child?

Since a parent is continually with a child, the spanking and emotions associated with it in our example become attached to the other infant (unless the parent is overly abusive, and then the fear may become solely attached to the abusive parent). If the parent is not overly abusive, the child as an adult may say, "I don't know what's wrong with 'them,' I don't think my folks ever disliked those kinds of people, yet when I get around them I always feel kinda scared, you know." We may not be able to remember that spanking in the presence of the "different" child but our emotions remember! And, that in turn affects how we act as adults.

We have been discussing fears. Some fears are actually very good, and it's a good thing we have learned their value. When I was a child I stood in wet grass and touched an electrified fence that kept the cows in. I got a painful shock and learned not to do that again. In fact, I became a little fearful when I got a bit too close to the fence and, come to think of it, so did the cows. And, when mother or father spanked or scolded us for playing in the street or playing with fire, fear kept us from doing these things again. The emotion of fear spread to the types of things we were spanked or scolded for and when we came into contact with them we thought twice. An alternative that works just as well is to use the parent's physical size to "loom" over the child, while simultaneously lowering your voice. At any rate, thank goodness mom or dad spanked or disciplined me for some of the things I did; I might not have survived without it.

Before we summarize this chapter, one more point needs to be made, and that is "immediacy." In order for emotions to be attached to appropriate stimuli, the response has to happen shortly after the stimulus has been presented. *Immediacy* is the key. (This is an important principle not only for classical conditioning but also for what we soon learn is called operant conditioning as well.) You cannot see your child playing in the street and ignore it and the next day spank or scold your child for playing in the street. About all the child learns in this case is that you often spank or scold him for what appears to be no reason. If you don't want your child to play in the street and you want the child to be fearful of doing so, you must apply the appropriate discipline *immediately* (and in the street).

There, that wasn't so bad, was it? And this is one of the tough chapters.

Things to Remember

1. Classical conditioning applies to lower animals and humans.
2. Through learning, we attach emotions to things, and, later, when we come into contact with these "things," they elicit the same emotion(s).
3. If you want your child to make an appropriate emotional attachment, you need to remember the idea of "immediacy."
4. Emotions that are elicited by particular stimuli or events can be changed.

3. Learning—Learning—Learning or Isn't My Little Girl Cute?

We begin this chapter the way that we began chapter 2, with animals. However, there is an important distinction here. In the previous chapter (when the animal was first learning the situation at hand), the animal responded *after* the bell was rung and the food was delivered. This chapter deals with a form of learning in which a response happens *before* the presentation of a stimulus (food, money, or praise). This kind of learning, which is commonly called operant conditioning, has been honed to a fine edge by the late B. F. Skinner of Harvard University.

The first concept, and one of the most important concepts we cover in this chapter, is that of "positive reinforcement." Basically, when some behavior leads to a positive reinforcer, that behavior will increase in frequency. The key is positive reinforcement. A positive reinforcer is something pleasant or something that the person likes, wants, or needs. There are two basic kinds of positive reinforcement. The first is called primary, and the other is secondary. Primary reinforcement refers to things that are associated with the basic needs of the person, and they are not thought of as being learned. Food and water are two of the most basic primary reinforcers. Secondary reinforcers are those that are *learned*. Initially they are associated with a primary reinforcer, and by this initial association they acquire their reinforcing properties. Money is an excellent example of a secondary reinforcer, and children quickly learn that it can be exchanged for food, soda, or almost anything they want. You cannot eat or drink money, but look what people will do to acquire it!

There are a lot of common reinforcers. We all like to eat when we are hungry, stay warm when we are cold, and drink water when we are thirsty. These are just a few of the basic reinforcers. But there are even more *secondary* reinforcers. These include a pretty dress, a new pair of shoes, a date (although a date may have some primary reinforcing properties), a new car, and so on down the list. However, we shall see that one of the most powerful reinforcers is *attention*. That little glance or a chuckle from mom or dad reinforces more behavior than you could ever imagine. We will develop positive reinforcement in more detail throughout this text, but it is probably the single most powerful principle affecting behavior. The one fact that must always be remembered is that as different as many people are, their reinforcers are just as different.

The second concept is negative reinforcement. Basically, whatever behavior keeps something bad or something we don't like from happening, that behavior increases in frequency. (This is not punishment. We cover that in chapter 5.) A good example of negative reinforcement is my hot pot story. If I reach for a hot pot I'll probably burn my hand, so I have learned over a period of time (I am not always a quick learner) that if I use a pot holder the pan doesn't burn my hand. Now each time I reach for a pot that I know is hot, I stop something bad from happening to me by using a pot holder. Believe me, when I work in the kitchen, my use of a pot holder for hot pots has greatly increased in frequency. I have tried to use the danger of hot pots as an excuse to stay out of the kitchen, but my wife also understands the principles of negative reinforcement, and she bought me a batch of brand-new pot holders. Darn.

For another example, let's go back to the time when I touched the electric fence when I was young because I was trying to get back home (see chapter 2). I soon learned to stop getting a shock by taking a long blade of grass and touching the fence with it rather than with my hand. There was just enough moisture in the blade of grass for me to get a tiny tingle that didn't hurt, and it saved me from a full jolt of the fence. Whenever I came to the fence I was afraid of it because of the shock I once received (classical conditioning), but I learned to avoid the shock by using a blade of grass (operant conditioning).

As you might suspect, most human learning situations contain aspects of both classical and operant conditioning. We need to be mindful of this fact in later chapters, particularly when we are attempting to change a child's behavior.

Positive and negative reinforcement are simple and yet so powerful that they have far-reaching consequences in the explanation of human behavior. Again, a few examples serve to drive home the point. A little girl is getting dressed in her frilly new dress. Her hair is combed, she has on her new bonnet and shoes and she thinks that she is pretty. She runs into the family room and says, "Daddy, Daddy, look at me." Under most circumstances, daddy tells his little girl how pretty she looks, gives her a hug, and so on. Daddy's attention is a positive reinforcer, and for a child parental attention is a very powerful reinforcer. What will happen to the frequency of the little girl's behavior? You guessed it. Daddy will see more of it. This is an example of positive reinforcement.

In the course of this text we use many examples to make the child-rearing process a little clearer. Our aim is to get the reader to start thinking about child-rearing in terms of the principles of learning.

We aren't born knowing right from wrong, or anything else, and we aren't born afraid of anything. If we were, all people would exhibit exactly the same fears and the same moral values. This is clearly not the case. We *are* born, however, with a *capacity to learn*, and it is this learning that makes each of us a unique individual. We learn what's hot and cold, we learn to "go potty," to write, to read, to curse, and we learn what's right and what's wrong (although we will see later that it's sometimes more exciting and more reinforcing to do what's wrong). Finally we learn about sex and everything else.

If this is true, and a great many psychologists think that it is, then this *learning process* is crucial. Since learning is terribly important, that means we don't want television or some disinterested person *teaching* our child! By the time our children are about seven or eight years of age, most of the foundation on which they will build the rest of their lives is pretty well set. This means that being a parent is a *very serious responsibility*. It takes time, patience, and often a lot of sleepless nights. And, unfortunately, there are times when parents are not very popular. But that goes with the territory. Raising a child is no accident. Remember, a child is yours from the time he or she is born until the time *you* die! I'm not suggesting that child-rearing can't be fun. It's easily one of the most rewarding experiences of life. Every parent realizes that the child also becomes one small step toward immortality. Raising children is a lot of work and it's worth it, but it is no accident. Love for the child is very, very crucial, but there is a lot more to it than just that! Neither this book, nor any book, can try to answer every question about raising kids, but the simple act of loving will go a long way toward making you an effective parent.

By now, I hope you are beginning to grasp the urgent and important implications of learning, but hold on. There are a few more ideas that are essential for a practical understanding of the learning process. One such concept is that of successive approximations or, more commonly, "shaping."

Many behaviors cannot be learned by doing them just once. Human behavior is so complex that most things we do take years of practice. When you practiced the piano as a child, you didn't sit down the first time and play Beethoven. No way, it took years of practice. And even then, Beethoven might have had a stroke if he had heard you play his music. The same is true of learning to walk, talk, swim, ride a bike, and so on down through the long list of human skills, skills we have all learned with lots of time and practice. We start with a small piece of behavior, and if we practice it long enough, we learn and eventually become proficient at it. (The key, however, is practicing little parts of behavior over a long period of time until we have shaped the final desired behavior.)

One of the things we must remember, as parents or as potential parents, is to take our time and let the child learn a little at a time. Going too fast is a bad idea. After all, children are not adults; they have the rest of their lives ahead of them to learn. One thing that has always been very difficult for me to understand is why parents scream at their children on the soccer or baseball field about doing this or that incorrectly.

Once, at one of my son's soccer games, an irate father got so mad at his son that he jumped out of his chair and started to scream at his child and push him around because he wasn't doing exactly what his father wanted him to do. In no time the child was in tears. Needless to say, neither the child nor the father ever came back. We all felt sorry for that child. In chapter 5, we discuss how and when to correct your child, but for now, the real point that I want to make is that our kids are still "little." Just a few years ago they weren't even walking or talking. Now all of a sudden, we expect them to be seasoned athletes. In addition, we take them to so many activities and practices that the only thing they have time to do is become neurotic. Let's just let kids be kids. Be patient; things will come along. Just keep reading, and a lot of what you need to know, to help your child, will be spelled out for you.

A final topic for this chapter is that of "immediacy." You will recall that earlier we mentioned the importance of immediacy in relation to classical conditioning. Immediacy is also important in operant conditioning. Again, I offer some examples to get the point across, but that's part of being a college professor.

We bring a puppy home and everyone is delighted with this lovable little creature. The kids argue about who is going to sleep with the dog, what we are going to do with the puppy, who's going to feed it, and so on. Everyone thinks the puppy is great. After about a week or two, some of the newness is worn off. Then, one morning we get up to find a little puddle here and there, a pile here and there, and some of our patience is worn thin. At this moment, we've forgotten that the puppy is just like a little baby. When you first brought your new baby home, how many times did you change the diaper? If you were to ask a mother, she would probably tell you that they don't have numbers that high yet. We forget that this new puppy is just like a little baby. We must think, at least unconsciously, that our puppy has a bladder the size of a fifty-five gallon drum. Well, we're the "boss" and we'll soon show this puppy that these "puddles" and "piles" will not be tolerated. So, we call the dog and then when he comes to us wagging his tail (little does he know), we grab him by the scruff of the neck and put his nose in this puddle and that one, and also add a few piles. At that point some people even try to dropkick the dog out of the door and get a three-point field goal, especially if they have stepped in one of these puddles or piles.

The dog isn't dumb, and it is comical to watch someone trying to catch his or her puppy after using this approach. Unfortunately, for both you and the dog, little if anything has been learned by the dog about "going potty" in the house. What the dog has learned is the lesson of immediacy. If I called you and then immediately put your nose in your doo-doo, would you come to me if I called you again later? Probably not.

What you need to do is remember the lesson of the new baby and how often he or she went potty in his or her diapers. We need to watch the puppy closely and the minute it tries to go potty we immediately need to clap our hands loudly and say very loudly, "No!" You can wrap up a newspaper and swat it across the dog's backside. Remember that we are not trying to cripple the dog for life, so don't swing like you are trying to hit a home run. All that we are trying to do is to startle the dog. So let's be *gentle*. Then we need to take the puppy outside and watch him for a while. When he begins to go potty praise him "immediately." This method is much quicker than the "nose in it" method, and it's less painful for both you and the dog. And you won't have nearly as much trouble catching the dog when it is outside.

Some people put down newspapers inside the house when the puppy is small and then gradually move the papers toward the door and then outside. This technique is not too bad, but it is a technique that you don't want to use over a long period of time. In this case, what you are really telling the dog is that there is a "place" in the house that it is okay to go potty. The real lesson that we want to get across is there is *nowhere* in the house where it is "okay" to go potty. Also, the puppy, like the small child needs some shaping and a great deal of love and patience.

We return to humans for another example. A store is offering fantastic bargains, and you want to rush there and get in on the wonderful sales. However, after you get there, you can't find anyone to wait on you. You look and look but no one is there to wait on you. If this continues, you will probably get disgusted and leave. If this happens every time you go to the store, you will, in time, stop going to that store. What good are these fantastic bargains if you can't get someone to wait on you so you can take advantage of them? Without realizing it, we often do a similar thing when our kids ask us for something. Our child comes and asks us to fix or do something for him or her. When this happens, what do we often say to them? "Not now, later." And if the child persists we say "Later" a little louder. Like the store, what good are the great bargains if no one is there to get them for you? Now, we cannot always drop everything when someone asks us to do something, but if you are the type that rarely or never helps your child so that "later" never seems to get there, what behavior are you reinforcing in your child? You are reinforcing your child for not asking you for things or for asking someone else. Don't be surprised when the child is fifteen or sixteen and in trouble. Don't ask, "Why didn't you come to me?" You've spent over a decade or more reinforcing your child not to come and talk to you. There are times during adolescence when kids are difficult to communicate with, even when things have gone well until that time. You can help your child in these difficult times by reinforcing your child to communicate with you while he or she is growing up. When you stop what you are doing and help your young one, you are really doing two things. First, you are reinforcing your child to come to you, because when he or she does come and communicate with you, it is followed by "immediate" results. Then, when you have to say, "After a while" the child will know that, that "after a while" really will come. Remember this child is your own flesh and blood. If you aren't going to interact with the child, why did you have him or her? Secondly, when you take the time to help your child, what you are also telling the child is that you think the child is important, that the child means something to you. Although we discuss this idea in more detail later, the attention that you give when one of the kids asks you to help goes a long way in helping your child develop a good feeling about his or her self-worth. The point is, if your child asks you for something, stop and try to do it, especially when your child is small. Encourage your child to develop a pattern of coming to you, and when you really do have to say "later," it will be okay because the children know that the "later" will come.

Although there are a few more ideas that we need to know, we have enough now to get started. As we develop behavior patterns that require other principles of learning, they will be introduced at that time.

Things to Remember

1. Behavior is learned.
2. Behavior that is positively reinforced will increase in frequency.

3. Behavior that stops something we don't like will also increase in frequency.
4. Primary reinforcers are associated with basic biological needs.
5. Secondary reinforcers are learned and built off of primary reinforcers.
6. Both primary and secondary reinforcers have a powerful influence on behavior.
7. Complex human behaviors are learned a little at a time—shaping.
8. If we want reinforcers to be effective we must use them—immediately.

4. How It All Gets Started

This is the last of the "hard" chapters. If you have read this far, the rest of the reading is a "piece of cake."

The minute we are born, we start a journey of learning that lasts until we breathe our last breath. Some psychologists have even argued that the birth process itself is important in shaping the personality of a person. That argument is a bit beyond the scope of this book, but the minute you are born you are interacting with your environment and that interactive process is the start of *you* and the development of *your* personality.

If all goes well, we are wrapped in a warm blanket and not too long afterward we start to receive food. When we arrive home we are the center of attention. Being the center of attention often disrupts the child's schedule, as most mothers will tell you. Sometimes it seems like the entire world wants to see the new baby. To save yourself some trouble, put your baby on a schedule that works for you and your child. If parents, grandparents, or neighbors want to see the new arrival, don't feel bad about telling them to wait until the baby is awake. If not, when they're done looking at the baby and go home, you are the one left with a baby that is cranky and tired, and it may take a while to get the baby back on schedule. Once in a while this isn't so bad, but when this happens several days in a row, *you* are the one who is up all night and day trying to get things back on schedule. What do you feel like when someone wakes you up at 2:00 or 3:00 A.M. night after night and your schedule gets messed up? The baby is no different. We at least understand why we are up (sometimes). Even so, we usually aren't friendly if it happens too often. What do you think happens to the baby? I'm sure the baby doesn't know why his or her schedule is messed up, but after a few of these wake-up times, you are the one who will pace the floor with the new arrival. I am belaboring this point because a baby on a regular schedule, even with some occasional disruptions, is a happy baby.

In terms of the learning patterns discussed in chapters 2 and 3, these interactions are written on the child's mind. This includes the patterns of behavior and the emotions associated with them. If someone wakes you every four hours and feeds you, or you are fed only when you awake yourself and cry, you are already learning about your environment and patterns of reinforcement that are starting to shape your personality.

Over the years, some parents have asked which feeding pattern is better. "Should I use a demand schedule or an hourly schedule for feeding?" Actually, there is no right answer to this question. It is better to ask yourself, what feeding schedule best fits into the world you have created for you, your mate, and the baby? What worked for your parents or friends, however well it worked, may not necessarily work for you. If you have any unusual or persistent problems, call your pediatrician or family doctor. But remember, it's your baby and your life. Don't put a strain on the adjustments that you and your mate are already making with this little bundle of joy.

Let's closely examine what is happening with the feeding process and part of the baby's nervous system. Although it will take us off of our main topic, I think you will find the information useful and it will give you a better understanding of what is happening inside both you and your newborn. These first few months are pretty well consumed with basic feeding, changing soiled diapers, and bathing the baby. First, as the baby eats and begins the digestive process, this plugs in the parasympathetic nervous system. Before we develop this idea, let's look briefly at the two main nervous systems of the human body.

Now, don't get excited. It is not all that difficult and you won't have to take a quiz over this material. Basically, there is the central nervous system, which is made up of the brain and spinal cord. The other major nervous system of the body is called the peripheral nervous system. This lies outside of the central nervous system (hence the term peripheral) and is divided into several different divisions. One of these divisions is the autonomic nervous system. This system is further divided into two basic parts—the sympathetic division and the parasympathetic division.

Whenever we are frightened or upset, the sympathetic division is operative and our body is actually ready for fight or flight. This is an old mechanism that was very helpful for basic human survival back when we were in the wild. When this system kicks in, digestion stops, our senses become sharper, more blood flows to the muscles, and adrenaline is pumped into the body. When this happened in the wild, we were ready to fight or flee for our lives. Have you ever noticed how upset your stomach is when you are nervous, anxious, or angry? Your sympathetic nervous system is engaged and the food just sits there like a concrete block. Many decades of extensive research has been done on the effects of prolonged exposure to your own sympathetic nervous system. While this system may have been great when we had to fight or flee from a saber-toothed tiger, it has caused many problems in a civilized society. In our highly technological world, it isn't the call of the wild that activates the sympathetic division, it's *stress*. When we do not handle stress appropriately, it overengages and activates the sympathetic division. This in turn leads to ulcers, hypertension, and a host of ugly and physically harmful conditions. We return to this line of reasoning in a moment.

The parasympathetic division has an opposite effect (hence the term *para* before the word *sympathetic*). When we eat, it engages the parasympathetic division and a by-product of the whole process is a more relaxed feeling. This is also (as we see in chapter 9) the nervous system that is associated with the initiation of sexual activity.

Some people actually use the forced engaging of the parasympathetic nervous system to help them indirectly handle stress. The scenario goes something like this: we have some stress, but we don't handle it directly because we haven't learned to handle it directly. This often is the case for women in our society. Our society has not reinforced females to be aggressive. If a woman is upset with her mate, she may not be able to get rid of her stress (he is a lot bigger and stronger or we teach "ladies" not to be aggressive), so she goes to the refrigerator to find something to eat. This eating forces her body to digest the food as best it can. While it is doing the digesting, the parasympathetic system is engaged and the person is a bit more relaxed. But when the stomach is empty and the stress is still there because we really haven't dealt with it directly, what do we do? We go back to the refrigerator and keep our tummies filled to keep the parasympathetic nervous system plugged in. If this vicious cycle isn't stopped, we create even more health problems because we will become *overweight*. To handle stress one must go to the source. If not, the stress stays and over time only gets worse.

Now, let's go back to feeding the baby. When this occurs the baby's parasympathetic nervous system is working. From a classical conditioning point of view, let's examine what is happening (remember, this is the type of learning that deals with emotions). While the baby is eating, it is being held, touched, and often talked or sung to. It doesn't take a genius to see that these stimuli are being associated with a positive feeling the baby has because it is eating. Again, we psychologists are in favor of breast-feeding. What have you got to lose? It can help the child emotionally and it sure beats getting up at night to warm up bottles.

If for some reason you can't breast-feed your child, be sure that you hold your baby at feeding time and the baby will still get a start on making the right kind of emotional attachments. This goes for you too, dad. You can hold a bottle just as well as mom can, and all of the emotional benefits can still be gained. But hold your baby! Don't go to K-Mart and buy one of those things that you can stick the bottle through and prop it up so that the baby can eat all by itself. While the parasympathetic nervous system is plugged in for this child, little if anything is being associated emotionally. This child is not getting much of an emotional start at birth. Hold the little one when you feed him or her!

In time, as the baby begins to get a little older, it begins to build the emotional foundation on which it will build its entire emotional life. This all starts with that early feeding and care. Have you given your child enough of a foundation on which to build a healthy personality? Or perhaps the best your child can do is pitch a tent that will represent its personality. If so, any storm of life can easily topple that structure. Notice how important just feeding the baby is in terms of personality development.

As I have grown older, one of the things I regret the most is that I didn't hold my kids more. Believe me, I held them a lot, but if I could, I would have held them even more. That time of holding, as I look back, was much too brief. Do it all you can whether your child is a girl or a boy. It won't make the boys sissies, it will make them emotionally healthier.

Things to Remember

1. The sympathetic nervous system is associated with stress, as well as the fight-or-flight response.
2. The parasympathetic nervous system is associated with a relaxed state.
3. Events in our lives become associated with and can trigger the sympathetic or parasympathetic nervous system.
4. Give breast-feeding an honest chance.
5. Be sure to hold your baby when you feed him or her.

5. How to Punish Effectively

One of the most frequent questions that I've been asked as a psychologist has to do with the use of discipline. On the surface, discipline appears to be a very simple thing, and yet it is one of the most difficult areas, especially when working with children. This is true partially because many parents are angry when they try to discipline their child and in part because of what they do after they have finished disciplining their child. It is extremely difficult to write about disciplining because it is so complex. You will understand this process and some of its associated problems after you have finished this chapter.

First, we discipline children so that they will have self-discipline when they are adults. Some people must think that when you graduate from high school or turn twenty-one somehow you are automatically ready to accept adult responsibilities. This is not so. In order to have the discipline to get up each day and go to work, and do all of the other things we must do to survive in this complex world, we must start shaping these responsibilities when we are little.

Secondly, if children do not have discipline or proper training, the seed for the "respect of others" will not be planted. If our culture is to continue, then we must discipline our children. Since World War II there has been a growing air of permissiveness. On the surface, the approach called permissiveness appears that we are being kind to our children because we let them do what they want to do so they will learn. In fact, we are doing them a grave injustice, not only for them directly, but for our culture as well.

I'm not advocating beating children. That would be even more horrible. What I am advocating is discipline applied appropriately, and for the proper reason. If you trace history back to Hammurabi's Code, the Ten Commandments, or early Roman law, you will note that some form of law (discipline) has always existed. It is the weave that holds the fabric of society together. But what we need is a humane system of discipline that is effective and leads to a healthy caring adult.

When we talk about discipline, most people conjure up thoughts or mental pictures about "hitting" their kids, and certainly this is one form of discipline. But discipline comes in many varieties. It can also include: (1) taking away privileges or (2) imposing restrictions on the child. However, since most people think of discipline as some form of spanking, let's begin with this perspective.

Don't even think of spanking a child before he or she is at least a year old or so. And *never, never* spank a child when you are angry. When I say spanking in terms of a child this young, I'm talking of something very gentle, very gentle. Sometimes a little slap on the hand (if he or she is getting into something) or a "gentle" slap on the diapered bottom in conjunction with a sharp verbal "No" is usually quite sufficient. In fact, just the parent's angry face is often enough to trigger the right behavior in most children.

Also, *never* hit a child in the head, no matter what the age. Most people don't realize how strong they are and that they can cause permanent brain damage. *Never, never hit a child in the head!*

When you spank a child, spank the child where God put that extra padding. Also, never use anything on your child's bottom but your hand.

The following ten points should be considered when you use punishment. I call them the Ten Commandments of Punishment.

1. The punishment must fit the crime.

If you make the punishment too mild, it will have little effect on the behavior that you want to change. Also, if it is too severe for a small infraction, it may produce a number of side effects, one of which is aggression.

Before we develop the two subpoints from this category, an interesting philosophical idea underlying punishment should be considered. It is based on an old Greek idea and is called hedonism. Basically, the idea states that we are driven by pleasure. Although this is a simple idea, a few moments' reflection will show that there is an awful lot to this simple idea. Think of the things that you like to do or the things that please you. For some it is eating, playing some sport, frequenting a bar, enjoying sex, dancing, working on your hobby, or whatever. For these "pleasurable things," do we have to force you to do it? Of course not. The idea of punishment is certainly very related to hedonism. The punishment we institute detracts from pleasure and the idea is that when we do something that leads to punishment, we will not do it again because the punishment we received takes away some of our pleasure.

This certainly is an entertaining idea, except that it does not explain all behavior. If punishment worked every time and if hedonism was the only guiding principle of human behavior, then prisons would clearly be much more effective than they are. Yet, in our culture, even the idea of the type of punishment you get for your crime is based on hedonism. If you do a little crime, you get a little punishment. As the severity of the crime goes up, so does the severity of the punishment. The idea is that you should have just enough negative residual left over so you won't commit the crime again.

At any rate, in order for your punishment to be effective, whether you use some form of spanking or take things away (no TV or friends over to play), the punishment must match the crime. Don't half kill the child for not finishing all of his peas or just frown if your child comes home with all "Fs." This will either make your punishment ineffective or it will lead to resentment, confusion, and anger on the part of the child.

Another aspect of making the punishment fit the crime is often misunderstood by many parents. Most books that talk about discipline rarely cover this difficult next point: don't use punishment for withdrawal behavior or aggressive behavior. For example, let's say that a fellow is calling his dog (dog has withdrawn) and when the dog finally comes, he beats the dog for not coming sooner. That doesn't make sense. Neither does it make sense for a parent to use spanking for a behavior of withdrawal. For example, you are calling your child (child is withdrawn) and when the child finally comes you beat the child for not coming sooner. It wouldn't make sense. Would you come? (A number of things can be done and we will develop these alternatives as we progress through the book.)

You should not try to get a behavior from a child that is contrary to the punishment you are using. You can't use a punishment system that evokes the very behavior you are trying to eliminate. The punishment makes the child want to withdraw from you so you spank him for not coming which in turn makes the child want to withdraw. Again, it doesn't make sense and it is not going to be a very effective system for you as a parent. Actually, in the case of the withdrawal, a positive reinforcement approach is much more appropriate. You take a behavior that the child is exhibiting and with positive reinforcement you begin to mold and shape the desired nonwithdrawal or approach behaviors (remember we discussed this in chapter 3). Can you imagine punishing a child for being shy by spanking him? Again, that doesn't make sense. Use positive reinforcement and begin to shape the behaviors you want and continue the reinforcement until the behavior demonstrates an increase in frequency, that is, until you are getting the pattern of behavior that you want.

Another problem is using spanking, a form of aggression, to eliminate aggression in children. Here you are modeling for the child the very behavior you are trying to eliminate. This tends to send a mixed message to the young child. You are giving strong aggressive examples of the very behavior you don't want the child to exhibit. Actually, for the child's aggressive behavior a more effective approach is to use a "time-out" procedure. In using the time-out approach it may appear that you are actually ignoring the aggression, but in the long run this is a more effective approach than showing the child how to be more aggressive with your aggressive modeling behavior. With the time-out, the child is not permitted to continue what he or she was doing. This time-out is seen as quite aversive by the child and in simple words, the child does not like it because it is boring and there isn't anything to do. By using the time-out procedure, the child is removed to a place where there is little stimulation. There is no telephone, television, radio, tape recorders, friends, or anything else (a chair at the dining room table, where no one will interact with him or her). As a general rule, when you start the time-out session it should last one minute for each year of the child's current age. Use this as a starting point and adjust if necessary. If this isn't working and the behavior continues, the next time-out session should be slightly longer. By the time the child has spent a half-hour to three-quarters of an hour at this (don't go beyond this period of time), this can be very aversive to the child. I have used this approach on my very social daughter and believe me, it works. Remember, whatever behavior terminates an aversive stimulus, that behavior increases in frequency. What terminates the aversive stimulus (the time-out)? A display of nonaggressive behavior by the child terminates the aversive stimulus. This ends up being more effective, and with appropriate application will greatly decrease the incidence of the unwanted aggression.

You are probably wondering if I approve of physical punishment. YES! But, it must be applied appropriately and at a time when you are not angry. Remember, we do not want to hurt or maim this child; we just want to change this child's behavior. The real question is, what is most effective for what we are trying to do? Sometimes a spanking is the very best thing you can do, but sometimes it is not the best thing you can do. And when you are angry is no time to make this decision. However, punishment is usually warranted if the child's behavior is harmful to himself or others, and must therefore be stopped quickly (e.g., a child playing in the street or hitting his brother or sister with something that could cause the child harm).

2. Punish immediately.

We once again consider the importance of immediacy. Punishment works best when it is applied as soon as the undesirable behavior has occurred. When punishment is delayed, it can have a reduced effect and in some cases it may have no effect at all.

Some years ago, a young mother came to me with a problem. She stated that she "hit and hit my kid and it didn't seem to do any good. Doc, can you tell me if he's retarded?" I asked her to tell me what was happening and to give me an example of a situation in which she punished her child. As it turned out, she had an eight-year-old son who was rather large for his age and she was a woman of very small stature. She weighed approximately ninety pounds and her eight-year-old weighed nearly as much as she did. When she hit him, he just laughed at her. After a while she gave up and began to make a list of his "bad stuff," as she called it, and the time of day it occurred. At 5:30 P.M. when her husband came home she gave him the "bad list" and ordered him to spank the child. The father, trying to respect his wife's wishes, spanked the child for all of the transgressions that had occurred throughout the day.

This may come as a surprise, but this did not change the child's behavior. What it did was make the child dread his father's 5:30 P.M. arrival. It took a while, but we were able to set up a schedule of reinforcement for the mother and in time the behavior actually began to change. She found that withholding some of her son's TV programs, and not allowing him to have friends over or to stay overnight with a friend on the weekend were far more effective than spanking. The taking away of privileges was something she could apply immediately to her son's inappropriate behavior.

The moral of the story is you must punish the behavior right when it happens. Now, sometimes this is not possible to do. When this happens, you can increase the effectiveness of the delayed punishment by reinstating, as much as possible, the scene of the crime. It is not as good as immediate punishment, but it is far better than delayed punishment alone.

3. No hugs or kisses right after punishment.

Some parents, as soon as they are finished spanking or punishing the child in some way, go to the child and want to hug or console him or her. That's a No, No! Don't do it! What many children learn from this is that bad behavior ultimately leads to some kind of reward, and as a result the inappropriate behavior remains (and sometimes actually increases because it got the child the attention he or she wanted). When you punish the child, you should ignore the child for at least a half-hour or so before you begin to interact again with the child. You want the child to know that what occurred was not appropriate or acceptable and you don't want a repeat performance. After some time has passed, it doesn't hurt to go over the inappropriate behavior and be sure it is clear to the child what you want. At that point, however, it is time to drop it. I've known some parents who keep griping about a small transgression by their child day after day. Forget it, and go on to the good things that the child is doing.

Another serious problem with loving children right after they have been disciplined, especially if spanking is used, is that it may cause problems which are sexual in nature. If you have spanked the child and his or her bottom is still stinging, and you immediately hug or interact with the child, the child may associate the stinging bottom with being held and loved. Just think, if only one in a thousand children would make this wrong connection do you realize how many people that would make in a population of some 250 million? I am convinced that some sadomasochistic tendencies have started this way. So, after you have disciplined your child, leave the child alone for a while.

This third commandment of discipline has several interesting problems that can accompany it. I have worked with a few mothers, thank goodness it's been very few, who because they have weak egos coupled with poor marital relationships, couldn't stand having their child angry at them. If this is you, you won't be able to change your child's undesired behavior. In fact, it will probably become worse over time.

As stated before, being a parent is not a popularity contest and there *are* times when our children will be mad at us. However, in the long run, in order to teach our children what they will need to know in adult life, we have to hang on in the face of some occasional conflict. If you can't make it through those hard times, then set your own personal house in order first. It may mean getting you and your mate on the same track and it may mean seeing a psychologist to get the job done. These last two are not mutually exclusive events. If this is your problem, do something about it so that if you need to apply some form of discipline, for the child's own good, you can do it. If not, you may pass on to the child the same poor parenting techniques that you have and start the cycle all over again. A hurt or broken personality does not get better all by itself like a small cut or a broken bone. A personality gets better when we do something active about it. Sometimes that "something active" may mean seeking professional help.

4. Provide an example of appropriate behavior.

If you have applied some form of punishment and you have stopped the ongoing inappropriate behavior, you need to give an example of some acceptable behaviors.

If not, your punishment will not be nearly as effective as it could be. And the child (as in the example at the beginning of this chapter) will misbehave just to get your attention, especially if it's the only time he or she can get it.

It is true that punishment is the most powerful means of *suppressing* an undesirable behavior. But, if you want to *change* a behavior, you must reinforce a behavior that is different and incompatible with the undesirable behavior. Don't you want to do more than just stop an ongoing behavior? Don't you also want to teach the child the right thing to do? Think of all the people who are in prisons across the country. While they are there they aren't committing the crimes that got them there. But when they get out they often go back to what they were doing before. But now many of them are even better at it. If you want to teach an appropriate behavior, you must step in after the inappropriate behavior is suppressed and reinforce the correct behavior with positive reinforcement. That's how you really change behavior! It works!

This approach also makes sense before you have to initiate some form of punishment. It is much easier to create an environment in which children will have less chance of misbehaving than to spank or holler at them every time you turn around, because their world is full of things that get them in trouble. For example: it is much easier to put away the expensive knickknacks that have been lying around the house than to spank little Johnny continually for touching them. Kids are naturally curious. In fact, curiosity is a good sign of intelligence and we don't want to stop the growth of intelligence. If you use only spanking or hollering, you may really be thwarting the child's natural curiosity. This can have a detrimental effect on his or her IQ development later, and you surely don't want to do that.

Consider this alternative. Put the precious breakable things away. As the child grows a little older, slowly put them back out. As you are doing this, let the child help you and let the child know that he or she can see the things when one of the parents is present. If the child wants to see one of the knickknacks, let him or her know that you must be present. If you bring these precious things out a little at a time with the sturdiest ones first, you can gradually shape a behavior pattern in the child that is acceptable. Too often we think of changing a child's environment after the "crime" has been committed. If you think ahead a little, you can save yourself a lot of grief and you won't thwart the child's natural curiosity. Of course, if a situation occurs that you can't prethink, then, after you are done with your punishment, be sure to allow for an alternative form of behavior that will not lead to punishment. Sometimes it is hard for us to think that behavior happens *in an environment.* You can become an environmental engineer and so structure the child's environment into one in which the child naturally behaves, because it's difficult not to. As the child matures, you can use your engineering skills to help the child and yourself to create a world in which it is easier to behave than to misbehave. Children are not bad; they are merely actors in their environment. If we remember to set the stage properly, we will have an outstanding performance.

5. Don't punish the child for not being old enough to know better.

An easy example would be to punish a five-month-old child because it is still going to the bathroom in its diaper. Most parents do not know that a child cannot control the sphincter muscle of the bladder until the nerves that command the muscle are myelinated. This is a fatty covering that surrounds and insulates the nerve much the same way the rubber coating on a lamp cord covers and insulates the electric wire. The process of myelination is complete at about eighteen months of age. After this myelination process has occurred the child can actually control the bladder and, of course, start to learn to control when he or she goes potty. I have often heard of the parent who had a child potty-trained at twelve months of age. Not so. What often happens in a case of this type is that the parent has the potty schedule memorized so it "appears" that the child is potty-trained. The point is that you cannot expect a pattern of behavior that the child is not capable of performing.

This example requires a word of caution. Even though the child may be ready neurologically at about eighteen months of age, most children are not really ready to get serious about being potty-trained until they are about two and a half to three years of age. So relax. Don't force the child to do something that he or she is not ready to do, especially since improper or overly harsh potty training can have some very serious side effects.

Another example is that we sometimes punish a child for not "knowing better." Not knowing better or thinking ahead is not a normal conceptual approach taken by young children. They must be of a certain age before they can conceptually be ready to think about a possible future outcome. I've known at least a few adults who still need to learn that lesson. If you try to teach this lesson to children who are too young, you are asking for something that they are not mentally able to do at that stage of their lives.

A final example is the ridiculous discriminations that parents sometimes expect their child to make. If the child curses just a little for Uncle John, the parents think it's cute, but if the minister is over and the child curses, it isn't so funny. The child can't discriminate between Uncle John and the preacher. To the child it's just another outsider. Although that is but one example, we as adults often ask children to make subtle discriminations that they are not ready to make. Before you get excited about an inappropriate behavior on the part of the child and want to punish the behavior, be sure that you aren't asking the child to make a judgment that the child is not yet able to make.

6. Punish the behavior, not the child.

This is another one of those areas in which parents often miss the boat. As bad as the child is and as angry as you are at him or her, your child should *always* know he or she is loved. If you are going to goof on one of these points, don't goof on this one. Feeling unloved is an awful feeling, and the later effect on adults' perceptions of themselves and their behavior can be disastrous.

One of the hardest things for a psychologist to do is to convince adults that they have self-worth. Many bricks build a person's self-worth, and I believe that feeling loved by a parent is one of them. Do not make the child's behavior a condition for your love and affection. What you may be teaching the child is that love is something that has to be earned. Love should be given unconditionally or it is not love. Don't say, "If you don't do this mommy and daddy won't love you." This approach starts a child on a journey that often cannot be stopped. Certainly, if the child is acting inappropriately, the behavior must be stopped, but don't do it by withholding love; you do it by changing the child's behavior. When your kids are knee-deep in trouble, there should be a foundation present in them that knows, even though they are in trouble, that you still love them.

7. Don't spank after adolescence has started.

By the time a child reaches adolescence, almost always some form of physical punishment will not change his or her behavior. It can also lead to undesirable side effects that are not healthy for the child in the long run. With some early maturing kids, this effect can occur even earlier.

Hitting or spanking a child who is of this age will lead nowhere. It just won't work! You have had some thirteen years to build your relationship and rules of the house with this child. If you haven't succeeded by now, the hitting at this age will only drive you apart and will often lead to a runaway child. In this crazy world today, a young adolescent on his or her own can be in serious trouble. Far too many young children are kidnapped, sexually abused, and sometimes even killed. You don't want this happening to your child!

If you are still having trouble with your child's behavior at this age, it's time to call in a professional (hopefully if there has been a serious problem you will have called a professional long before this). That doesn't mean everything can be resolved overnight, but you can start on the road to a healthier child and a better relationship. Seek out a professional with your child. You may not want to face the alternatives. In any case, it is too late for physical punishment and for the older child other approaches are needed.

8. Be consistent.

Don't spank your child for something he or she does one time and then think that it is cute and laugh when the child does it again. This kind of parental behavior can really mess a kid up because he or she never knows where he or she stands. Research has clearly demonstrated that a child is better off psychologically in a home in which there is very strict discipline than in a home in which there is inconsistent discipline. This doesn't mean that I want you to be overly strict with your child, but it does point out that consistency is very important. Children will always test their limits and your consistency (sometimes I think it's an innate thing God has given kids), but this is normal. There are times when you, by a frown or by grounding or whatever, have to cement the fact that there are clear-cut boundaries and that these boundaries are consistent.

Without consistency your child never knows what is what or where he or she stands. In their confusion, they aren't happy, we as parents aren't happy, and it's a constant battle. Be consistent.

9. Follow through.

Closely associated with point 8 is the idea of following through when you punish a child. Unless you are ready to do what you say, *don't say it*. For your child's behavior to change it has to have a consequence. If you threaten the child with no television, no phone privileges, or being grounded, you *must* carry out your threat. If you don't, your child will know that your threats don't mean anything. Now, if you find you have been unrealistic with your punishment, or that something different happened than what you thought happened, it is time to revise your punishment. This point is very important and is worthy of some further explanation.

Since we parents are human, we make mistakes. It's okay to do so, but when we find that we have goofed we need to go to the child and say that we were wrong and we are sorry. If we don't, our kids often learn that we aren't fair in our dealings with them. And will they tell you when you are not fair! This is another thing that can cause them to have a bad image of themselves.

What happens over a long period of time is that they begin to think very little of themselves. You didn't think enough of them to bother to apologize when you were wrong, so why should they think much of themselves? If you are wrong, be big enough to admit it and revise or eliminate your punishment. It's a harder way to go, but in the long run you will have a much better relationship with your child and it is better for his or her mental health. I had to do this with my kids and believe me, my youngest daughter could make you feel lower than a rock at the bottom of the sea. It was hard to admit mistakes, but over the long haul your kids will respect you for it and they will learn to respect themselves.

In the extreme, I have seen some people continue a relationship that was psychologically unhealthy for them. They have the idea that they aren't worth much and don't have the right to ask for anything better so they better stay because they aren't worth anything, and something else might be even worse. Because of the double standard we have had in our culture, I have seen some women stay in an unhealthy situation that a man wouldn't put up with for ten seconds. (This is obviously tied very closely to point 6: Punish the behavior, not the child.) Again, children must always feel that they are loved and that they are worthy of being loved. Since this point is very important, we will touch on this discussion several times throughout this book.

10. Be united.

Children are exquisitely sensitive if there is any inconsistency between mom and dad. Before you decide on a plan of attack, have your forces together. If not, your weaknesses will be exploited and you will lose. Your little one, who can't figure out very much, becomes a military general with a winning strategy. Don't argue in front of the child over what is right or wrong in terms of his or her behavior, or what reward or punishment is going to be used. Work out your plan ahead of time and stick to it, if you are right. Never argue over rewards or discipline in front of your kids or it will be kids 1, parents 0.

There is a hidden agenda with this point. That is, you and your mate have a relationship such that you can communicate with each other and the two of you aren't involved in a power struggle. If you have a problem in one of these areas and you are not getting along with your mate, then the children's "bad behavior" may be a reflection of your interpersonal difficulties. It isn't going to work smoothly unless you handle your own problems first. Again, if professional help is needed, seek it. Quit talking about it with your friends and do something effective about it.

Why is so much emphasis put on discipline, and why is it so important? If you don't keep order in your house so that some rules and authority have some meaning, how am I as a teacher going to keep order in my classroom so learning can take place? And, as children who haven't learned the right way to act get older, how can we keep order in our society? It all begins at home with you as parents. Do kids today respect authority and respect the rights of others? It all begins at home with you!

At this point we have looked at the Ten Commandments of Punishment. An illustration of punishment will, I hope, make some of this come to life. We start with a little boy who lives in a home in which both parents work. When both parents come home at night, Junior runs over to dad to show him what he has done at the day-care center. But dad is tired and despite Junior's pleas, the father tells him to go away because he is tired and he will look at the work Junior has done, "later" (in chapter 3 remember the problems that occurred when a parent said, "Later"). Receiving little reinforcement from dad, Junior goes into the kitchen (actually dad should be in there also) and desperately tries to get mom's attention. Unfortunately, he meets the same fate with her, and it appears that no one will give Junior some attention and look at his work. Finally, he begins to play and begins to make so much noise that dad can't watch the news on television. Finally, dad gets up to show Junior who is boss in the house and to quiet him down.

Now, dad thinks that he has shown Junior that when he says to be quiet, that is *exactly* what he means! Unfortunately, what the little boy has actually learned is if he wants attention from his environment, what he has to do is disrupt it. Some kids want attention so bad that they are willing to risk a spanking for it. A spanking, after all, is a form of attention and (if that's all there is) it may become the reinforcer. If this pattern continues, imagine what the little boy will be like in grade school. One can picture a grade school teacher trying to keep all thirty of the kids busy, and here is Junior, not getting enough attention. What pattern of behavior does Junior know? You guessed it. He begins to bother those around him and seek attention by disrupting his environment just like he does at home. The teacher goes over to him and starts to holler at him, but unfortunately she is actually reinforcing the very behavior that she wants to get rid of. And with the other students watching, Junior's disruptive behavior is not going to decrease, but increase.

Discipline in its various forms is certainly needed by developing children. A pat on the rump or a sharp word at the right time sounds like a simple, straightforward action that even a young child can easily understand. But be careful; there are times when you may actually be increasing an undesirable behavior instead of decreasing it.

Things to Remember

1. The punishment must fit the crime.
2. Punish immediately.
3. No hugs or kisses right after punishment.
4. Provide an example of appropriate behavior.
5. Don't punish the child for not being old enough to know better.
6. Punish the behavior, not the child.
7. Don't spank after adolescence has started.
8. Be consistent.
9. Follow through.
10. Be united.

6. Making Things Easy

There are two basic things that I want you to learn in this chapter. One is to learn what an S^D is and the other is how to make a simple graph that will help you. An S^D stands for discriminative stimulus. Basically, an S^D is a stimulus or some stimulus situation (a signal or a cue) that has come to represent certain consequences, or to stand for certain things because of our learning experience with them. Let me use a common example that I often use in class. When you were a small child growing up, how many times did your mom holler at you for something? Most students will say that "mom" used to scream and scream. And when her voice reached double A above middle C, you knew she was coming and it was time to move. Then I ask, "How many times did your dad holler at you?" Most students say, "Once!" There is a lesson here. It wasn't that dad didn't love us or that mom loved us more, but when dad said something once, we knew that there would not be a second time. From the very beginning we learned that dad hollered just once. But, mom would holler many, many times. An S^D takes on meaning when it has a consequence associated with it. You can make your job as a parent easy from the beginning by not saying something to the kids that you don't intend to follow up. If you are going to say a hundred times, "Take your feet off the furniture," and you never follow it up with a consequence (that translates into getting up and doing something about the feet on the furniture), all you are teaching your children is that your warnings or commands don't mean anything. And why should they bother reacting to warnings that don't mean anything?

To be sure, much of life is filled with warnings (S^Ds). If you drive down the road and see a red light, what do you do? You stop. If you see the middle amber light, what do you do? You speed up because in the past you have not had to stop when you did that. If you are sitting in church and your boyfriend starts hugging or kissing you, what would you do? You would feel uncomfortable because, in the past, the church has not been a prompt (an S^D) for such behaviors. If you were parked out on lovers' lane and your date suddenly dropped on his knees and started to pray, how would you feel? Pretty weird, I imagine. You might think that your kisses are great but not that great. Anyway, you would probably be startled because a date is not usually a prompt (an S^D) for praying.

Another common S^D is the telephone. A typical situation goes something like this. Mom picks up the phone and the kids go bananas. They have learned that when you are on the phone you won't put it down, and you can only move as far as the cord will reach. In addition, they know that when you say, "Be quiet," your "be quiet" has no consequences. You won't *do anything* as long as you are on the phone.

What you must do is say, "Be quiet," and make sure that the kids have heard you. After that, you don't say, "Be quiet," again. No indeed. Instead you follow it up with a consequence. Before long the kids learn that when you say, "Be quiet," it has some *meaning*. They learn that the meaning is be quiet or there *will* be a consequence. Kids are not born ignoring their parents. You have to teach them that. Instead of teaching them to misbehave, why

48

not teach them something that makes raising the kids easier? It all comes back to your parenting skills. What your kids know is what you've taught them.

The last example I'd like to develop is to make you, the parent, a prompt (an S^D) for communicating with your children. Let me explain. When your children come to you, do you answer them or do you just keep putting them off and never quite seem to get around to answering their questions? If you are guilty of behaving like this, then you are making yourself an S^D for *not responding* when your kids ask you to communicate or do something for them. As the years go by, don't be surprised if you have been very successful at convincing your kids that it's pointless to talk to you. You never respond. You never communicate. Always remember that behavior patterns are created and maintained because the behavior has had a consequence. If you want to keep communicating with your children, their communications with you must have a consequence, hopefully a reinforcing one. If it does, then in the future, when they want you to do something for them or want to interact with you, you *will* have the communication patterns that you want to have with your kids.

Now, let's figure out how to make a graph. Don't worry. You don't need a degree in math. What we will do is really quite simple. First, as you will see in Figure 6-1, there are two sides to a graph. Side A is called the vertical side or, more technically, the ordinate. Side B is called the horizontal side or more technically, the abscissa.

It is customary to graph the frequency (how many times something has occurred) on side A, and the variable or thing you are trying to measure on side B. For example, if one were to graph a thousand IQ scores, the number of IQ scores would go along side A, and the actual IQ scores would be graphed on side B. Figure 6-2 is an example of

Figure 6-1

Side A

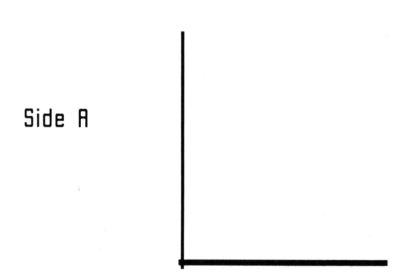

Side B

such a graph. As with many things, when one graphs IQ it forms a normal curve.

Now, let's look at a graph for weight loss over time. On side A we would plot the weight loss in pounds, and along side B we would plot time. Figure 6-3 gives you an example of such a graph.

The real key is to make the graph work for you or your child. Let's play with Figure 6-3 to make our point. If we stretch Side A to read only up to five pounds notice the difference it makes for a weight loss of three pounds (see Figure 6-4). If you change the graph (Figure 6-5) to read up to twenty-five pounds of weight loss, notice that in the first graph (6-4) the weight loss, even though it is small, appears to be very pronounced. But, in Figure 6-5 the weight loss of the same three pounds is hardly noticeable. When you make your graph, play with it (by using large spaces to indicate small changes) so you can easily see the progress your child is making. Make a small difference show up big on the child's graph and the child's progress will be rewarded. You might also want to play with the abscissa and see if it too will make a difference. Your goal is to have a graph that will help you in shaping or reinforcing the behavior you are after. There is nothing magic about how you make your graph, so make it work for you. In chapter 7 we see how to make a slightly different graph, but here too we make the graph work for us. Be sure to make the units on the graph big enough so that even a small amount of behavior change will be evident on the graph, and thereby reinforcing to the child, as well as to you. The graph makes changing behavior easy. Use it.

Grade school teachers often put a chart on the wall and paste stars on it for excellence in spelling, math, or whatever. As you might suspect, I certainly agree with this. But what about the child who can't ever get a star? How will this

Figure 6-2

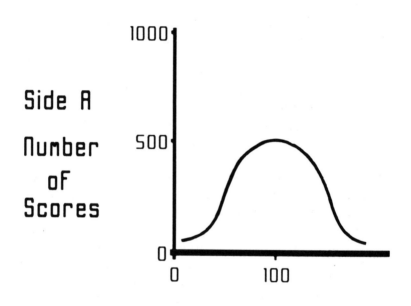

Side A

Number
of
Scores

Side B

IQ

Figure 6-3

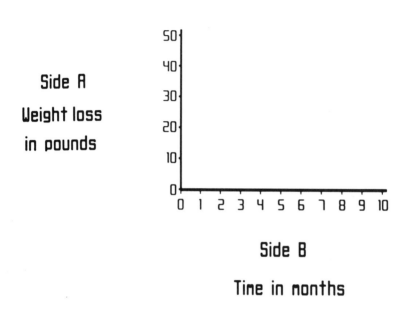

Side A
Weight loss
in pounds

Side B

Time in months

Figure 6-4

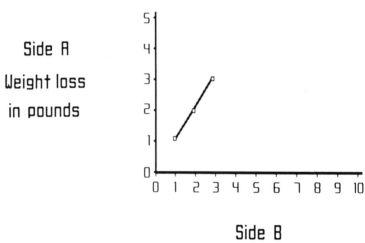

Side A

Weight loss

in pounds

Side B

Time in days

Figure 6-5

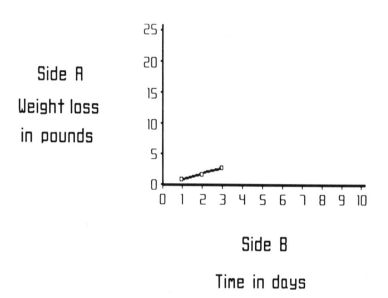

Side A
Weight loss
in pounds

Side B

Time in days

child perceive the stars? For most kids, the star approach is great. Some kids, however, don't buy into the system. For them, the chart with the stars becomes another thing in their world that reminds them how dumb they are. They are convinced that they can't do the work and they hate it, like so many of the other things that become associated with school. For these students, you should be creative enough so you can develop a system that they can find rewarding and you can slowly, over the course of the school year, pull them into the mainstream of the academic system. It happens because they succeed, and success breeds more success. You might start by making the chart *so easy* that they can't miss getting a star on it. Or make a chart that represents something they *can* do even if you think it's almost nothing, and then slowly, over time, demand more from the child. Try it. It works!

If we're building a system in education, let's work so that every child in the class can find something to be reinforced for, so that every child can feel good about himself or herself in an educational setting (remember classical conditioning). If we can do it, we'll be able to keep every child interested in school. We won't lose a child. Come to think of it, it is really scary how much "power" each parent and grade school teacher has. Caring for children is a serious responsibility, so use it carefully and well.

Things to Remember

1. An S^D is a prompt that acquires its meaning because of learning.
2. Use a graph to help your child learn a new behavior.
3. Make each learning step small enough so that the child will be successful.

7. Let's Change the Behavior

We will have to do two basic things in order to be able to change the behavior of a child. First, we will need to look at a conceptual approach of what we must do and, second, we have to learn the nuts and bolts of how to do it.

Let's take a brief look at what is involved in changing a behavior. The first thing that we must decide is what we want when the child-rearing is done. Technically psychologists call this specifying terminal or target behavior. That is, what do you want when you are done with the training: less talking, not playing with the food when a child eats, going potty on the pot, less fighting, eliminating the temper tantrums, or whatever. Before you start the training, you need to sit down and try to figure out exactly what you want. This system works, so be careful what behavior(s) you pick, because if it is a pattern of behavior that is possible for the child to do, the child will have the behavior. I'm sure you are familiar with the old bromide, "Be careful of what you dream because dreams come true." That really applies here. Be careful of the final behavior you select because with this system, if it is a behavior pattern that is within the child's potential, you will get it, if you follow the procedure correctly.

So what do you want? Actually, you probably have a long and interrelated list of what you want. Some of it will come quickly but other behaviors will take a whole *lifetime*.

For example, after the child is physically capable of speaking, you and the child will start to shape words, followed by the identification of objects and sentence building. However, such behaviors as being self-sufficient and responsible, or how to study, are behaviors that take many years to learn, and unfortunately some never learn them. Even so, within your hands as a parent, you hold the potential of shaping all these things. We return to this subject later.

The next thing to do on our list is to establish the baseline. What this means is that you are going to keep count of how many times the behavior is or, in some instances, is not occurring. Sometimes one wants to increase the frequency of a particular behavior and sometimes one wants to decrease the frequency of a particular behavior. How do we know if we've increased or decreased a particular behavior if we don't know how much of the behavior we are getting before we ever get started? So, we establish the baseline and then measure the behavior change from our baseline. An interesting thing about this is once you do this, you will occasionally see that the behavior is not occurring as much as you might have initially thought. In this case, no actual behavior change is really necessary. When we get to the nuts and bolts of actually changing the behavior, I'll show you how this is done.

Another thing that we need to do before we get started is determine the reinforcer. This seems simple on the surface, but like some of the other things that we have looked at, it is not quite as simple as it may first appear. First ask yourself what is reinforcing to you. Then ask yourself if these reinforcers are exactly the same things that are reinforcing to your mom or dad or mate or brothers and sisters or your friends. True, we share many common reinforcers but we also have things that are reinforcing to us and not to those around us, at least not in the same way they are reinforcing to us. Do not pick something that is reinforcing to you if you are trying to change someone else's behavior. If you want to change your behavior, then you pick something that is reinforcing to you, but if you are changing someone else's behavior, then you pick those things that are reinforcing to that individual. As the child's parent, you ought to know what is or is not reinforcing to your child. But, the best thing to do is to ask your child. Parents are often surprised at what is rewarding to their children. When you have determined the reinforcer, then you and your mate will have to decide how you are going to dispense the reinforcer. But, you must be in agreement on this.

Finally, you must apply successive approximations or shaping. Remember, Rome wasn't built in a day and neither are the complexities of human behavior. You start first with some simple pattern of behavior that the child is already exhibiting, and gradually in a step-by-step manner you start shaping or funneling the behavior in the direction of the target behavior. Also, parenting is much easier when we break down the target behaviors. That is, what you want the child to do is broken down into manageable "little chunks." This will make the following review list much easier to implement.

For a review you will:

1. Determine the target behavior you want in the child.
2. Establish his or her current baseline.
3. Determine the reinforcer (reward you'll use).
4. Use shaping (reward successive steps toward the target behavior).

Now, for a few examples. Let's start with potty training and cleaning up the child's room and then move on to temper tantrums. Finally we'll look at homework or study behaviors.

In the first example, we want our child to stop going potty in his diaper and start going potty in the toilet. Two quick ideas before we start this. First, not going potty in one's pants is not the same as going potty in the toilet. They are two separate behaviors, and we must treat them that way. Second, the child must be ready neurologically. You will remember that in chapter 5 we talked about myelination. Myelination occurs at about eighteen months of age. It is this myelination process that permits the infant to control its bladder. When this occurs the person can now control the sphincter muscle that permits the person to urinate on demand. I have occasionally seen well-meaning parents trying to train their child at an age when this myelination could not have occurred. Do not do this. It would make as much sense to say to someone, "Go outside and lift your car above your head." So, before you begin potty training you must be sure that myelination has taken place. I have taken the time and space to repeat this material because of its importance. In a later chapter we further develop the other implications of potty training.

So, how do you actually begin? Well, with some children just using the training pants and telling them that they are big just like mommy and daddy or big brother or sister is a great help. To be sure, it takes a lot more than this, but it's a step in the right direction. Another good starting mechanism is to make frequent but short visits on the "potty." Remember you do not want the child to just sit there for a long time. That's hardly reinforcing. For a small child, anything after about five minutes starts to be a long time. Also remember that we do not want children to associate anything that is bad with the bathroom.

I need to stop our line of reasoning for just a minute and mention some things that I have known some people to do that I do *not* want you to do. I once knew a lady who took a coat hanger and hung the soiled diaper around the child's neck for hours whenever her children went potty in their pants. Do not do this. I have known others who have made their child sit on the "potty" for hours or spanked their child severely for going in his or her pants. Again, do *not* do this. Some parents have the idea that their child is bad or doing this on purpose. This simply isn't true. Kids are not bad or trying to get you. They are learning a brand-new task and it is a difficult one. Just remember, a year or so ago they were not even alive. Relax and don't worry about what your neighbor or in-laws think. Remember classical conditioning. We don't want to associate negative emotions with the genital area. For some kids, this may really be a problem in adulthood. We don't want a boy to fear or think that the genital part of his body is dirty, evil, or whatever. The same thing holds true for the girl. Don't, just because you had to potty-train and punish your children, leave them with an image of themselves or their genitals that will be a problem for them in adulthood. What we want to shape is a healthy view of themselves sexually, physically, and psychologically. The potty training is but a small step toward our final goal. Don't get so wrapped up in this short-term goal that you lose sight of the final goal. Do you know any adults who potty in their pants? No. But, do you know adults who are messed up sexually? You would not believe how many sexual problems are started during potty training. Relax. There is no deadline for getting the job done. The real goal of potty training is to produce healthy adults who have a healthy view of themselves sexually. Kids are going to learn to go in the pot and not in their pants. For the sake of a few months one way or the other, don't you want a child who enters adulthood with a healthy and wholesome view of himself or herself? Sure you do. So relax and take it slow. Real slow.

Now, there is no magic that I or anyone can tell you about potty training. Just don't look at it as a test of wills, because it isn't. Remember, the child is learning two new tasks that are very difficult. One, don't go potty in the pants and the other is to go on the large white throne. These are two separate tasks. When you feel that the child is ready to make a lot of frequent trips to the pot, start the training. It is okay to express disappointment in the behavior, but you must also praise the child when it has had a dry diaper for a while and especially when the child goes potty on the pot. When the child goes potty the child should feel that he or she has just about done the greatest thing in the world. When the child is starting on this task the child will make many mistakes. We all make mistakes when we are learning something new. The problem with potty training is that the child can't hide the mistakes. Also, many children are afraid to sit on the pot because to them, the hole is so big they might be afraid of falling in. You will probably want to purchase a little chair with an old-fashioned pot under it or get one of those chairs that hook on to the top of the toilet seat. I would also recommend a small stepping-stool to be placed in front of the toilet. If children can put their feet on the stool, it may give them a feeling of security. For a small child, sitting on that "big toilet" can be scary. Don't make it a scary experience. Remember, do it in small, successful steps.

Another thing that you might want to try is a small chart that features one of the child's favorite animals. Have the animal (let's use a turtle for the sake of this example) start on the left side of the sheet of paper and each time the child goes potty on the pot or the diaper is dry you move the turtle closer to the goal. In this case, the turtle's goal may be a little pond, or if you draw a picture of your home, it will seem as if the turtle is coming to visit you. Each time the child has dry pants or goes potty in the pot, the turtle will get closer and closer to the goal. If the pants are wet, you might want to move the turtle one space back. Have the child help you move the turtle either forward or backward. Be sure to make each behavior step small enough so the child can be rewarded while also making each step on the chart large. When the turtle reaches the goal have a favorite snack for the child, praise him or her, or give the child something the child finds rewarding. Over time, we want the child to succeed, but as time goes by, we require more from the child to move the turtle closer. You might want a small subscale so that you can keep track of the number of times the child has to go potty or have dry pants. You might want to make a new chart every day for a week, then chart two days at a time. With each new graph, stretch the time just a little. Just remember, you must make the initial steps small enough so the child will be successful and be sure to share and enjoy the child's triumphs. (See figures 7-1 and 7-2.)

It is very important, and I cannot stress it enough, that the child feel *successful*. These small successes will accumulate and will lead to bigger success later, but we need something to build on in the very beginning. When you start, you might want to ask the child about every fifteen to twenty minutes if he wants to go to the pot and see if the pants are dry. Perhaps every half an hour ask the child if it is time to sit on the pot. Ask the child, and be sure that you have the child's attention. Do not nag the

Figure 7-1

Time in hours

Figure 7-2

Time in days

child and ask him or her many, many times, "Do you have to go?" No one likes to be nagged, and neither does the child. As time goes by, and the child becomes more and more successful, you will want to make longer and longer intervals between your "asking times." In this manner you can eventually shape yourself out of a job and the child will be assuming more and more control and responsibility for going potty. But, go slowly, very slowly. Even after the child has learned the task there will be an occasional mishap. Treat the mishap as an isolated incident, and not a failure to be potty trained. It is not the end of the world. Help the child clean up and talk about going to the pot. Again, do not nag the child.

Parents often run into another problem with this, especially if there is a new child or mom has gone back to work. All of a sudden you may find that you are back in the diaper business. If we scold, holler, and belittle the child, the situation usually gets worse. What to do? Stop a minute and think. When you were going through the whole business you were "spending time with the child." Besides learning when and where to go potty, the baby also associated the whole potty business with spending time with you. What you may be getting with the return of wet pants is not a forgetting of how to go potty, but a barometer that cries for more time with you. If you really want to solve the problem, spend more time with the child, that is, quality time with the child. That does not mean you are with the child when you're watching television. That usually is not quality time. It means that you do things with the child. Don't have time? Make time. I shall say this many times in this text and I don't mean to be preaching to you or nagging you either, but those first five to eight years are more important for the child's development than you might ever imagine.

Another little digression. I often hear parents say, "I want my kid to have the things I never had." You are kidding yourself. Give the child something that you can't buy. Give them *you*, the gift of your complete attention. In the long run it's far more important for their psychological development. Besides, when you do not spend time with the child and just always give, give, give, children learn what we psychologists call "learned laziness." As a result, they learn something about the world that just isn't true. They learn that you don't have to earn things, and they learn that if you will wait, the world just gives things to you. Why work for something? As children grow make them work for their allowance and they will learn that the world doesn't just hand things out. They also learn that if you have to work for things you usually take better care of them because it isn't just handed to you. Don't misunderstand me, I'm not saying that we shouldn't give things to our kids, but in our culture I think that we just "give" far too much, and we expect far too little in return. Tell me that's the real world. Clearly it isn't. In a few chapters we pick up this idea again, but for now we return to our original topic, potty training.

Potty training is not one of the joys of being a parent, but if you can just relax I promise you that your child will not get married going down the aisle wearing a wet sagging diaper. The key, of course, is to take it a little at a time and allow for some mistakes.

The next example that I would like to develop is teaching your child to clean up his or her room. I feel that this is one of the more important things your child will learn from your reading of this book. Let me go over some of the reasons for this before we begin, so that when we actually start with keeping the room clean, we won't have to make so many digressions as we did learning about potty training.

First, if you are a person who is a "slob" it is going to be hard to teach your child to keep his or her room or part of the room clean. Remember the old bromide, "like mother, like daughter; like father, like son." I think the idea can also be captured in "monkey see, monkey do." So, if you are going to teach your child to keep his or her room clean, that means that you too must set an example, and keep your room or your house in some semblance of order. There is actually a subpoint to this idea of keeping your house clean and it has to do with your mate and not the children.

It is difficult to share a home with someone who is a real slob. This is especially true if the individual's idea of cleaning up is to move a junk pile from one corner to another. This can put a real strain on the person who is concerned with keeping a clean and orderly house. I have had people tell me that they have felt like a slave to the slob. I have also known several individuals who have gotten a divorce because they got tired of always doing the cleanup. This does not mean that you must keep your house so sanitary that you could do open-heart surgery on the kitchen floor, but it does mean that you should try to keep your home at some reasonable level of order if you expect your children to do so.

The second point that I want to make in this section is that learning to keep your room in order may be one of the first steps in keeping your home and perhaps even your life in order. In adulthood, this can easily generalize to keeping our environment in order and not destroying it. At times when my family and I are out for our Sunday drive we often see people throwing all manner of things out of their car window. I often wonder what their homes must look like. To respect the world we live in, we must learn that respect at home as little children. This, then becomes the first step in shaping the terminal behavior of respecting our environment on a more global scale.

One final point. What a little girl can learn so can a little boy and vice versa. There are no jobs around the house that are just for "girls" or just for "boys." The tasks around the house are for all to do. After all, isn't all of the family living there? We don't live in a subsistence agricultural society anymore, where dad and the boys plow the fields and gather the crops while mom and the girls keep house and make the meals and can the food for the long winters. We live in a modern society where anyone can use a can opener and make a meal. But some still adhere to the old agricultural societal model. In a modern society in which both parents work and often at the same tasks, we need to be more equitable with the division of labor and the division of free time. So, let's start with the children and develop a model that will work better for a modern technological society. No more, "Honey, you can't do that 'cause it's only for boys," or "Son, you really shouldn't do that 'cause its really a girl's job." Just remember, whatever model they have in their heads about treating jobs around the house or how they relate to the other sex was put there by you. Why not put in a model that has a better chance of succeeding in our society and one that, I think, has a better chance of building a base for a real sharing relationship in adulthood? Who knows, it may be a first step in making marriages that last because they are based on two equal sharing partners, not a master and slave relationship. In those kinds of relationships the "slave" looks forward to someday being free. Additionally, a boy who can't cook or a girl who can't change a faucet washer is at a real disadvantage. Why handicap them?

I hope this does not come across as if I want you to stand over the kid and be sure that he is always busy cleaning up. I clearly do not mean that and I'm the first one to let kids be kids. The lessons I'm talking about are very small ones when the children are also small, and gradually, as they grow larger, they should be assuming more and more of the responsibility of cleaning up their room.

When they are very little, say two or three, kids are not mentally or physically ready or able to clean up the whole room. At first they can help you clean up the room. While you are doing this, you might want to tell them that when they are finished playing they should put their toys away. (Remember that childhood play is the foundation of adult work and play.) The same can go for clothes when the child takes them off. No one likes to pick up after an adult who just throws his or her clothes all over the place like a two-year-old. If you start with what the child can handle and make the steps small, the child will gradually grow into the pattern and won't even think a thing about it. To be sure, the cleanup or anything else you do is going to take you much longer, but the investment of your time in the child's development will pay dividends for the child for the rest of the child's life. Take the time; in the end you too will be rewarded.

Now, just because your children clean up their rooms doesn't mean that they are going to be neurotic or sissies. It does mean, however, that they are learning to assume some of the responsibilities for themselves. Remember, you eventually want to work yourself out of a job. Don't worry; they are not going to have their rooms ready for the Good Housekeeping Tour. We wouldn't want them to be that way. Kids are always going to be kids and that is actually healthy. But you can gradually help them assume the responsibility for cleaning up their room. As they get a little older, both the girls and boys can be in charge of the particular room, even a bathroom, as part of their household chores. Don't be too critical of the job. Remember, they are just learning, and the fact that they are even assuming the responsibility to do the job is a gigantic step. Think of the adults that still can't do that. Be gentle and take it slowly. Be sure to praise them for their good works.

One of the tough things that I've had to face is when your child has someone over to play and when the friend leaves, you go into your child's room and it looks like a project for urban renewal. What to do? It is not fair to scream at your child and make him or her tackle the Herculean task alone. In the future, when the child who helped make the mess comes over, be sure to watch the clock and stop the children, say twenty minutes early, and be sure they clean up the room. At first you may have to assist, but (as usual) you want to work yourself out of a job. If that particular child who comes to visit refuses to help clean up, you will have to restrict the child's visits or restrict what the child can play with or do when the child does come to visit. This is usually not all that hard. What becomes hard is when you have relatives over and their kids help to make the mess and then they run to their mommy or daddy so they won't have to help your child clean up. You might suggest that since "both" children made the mess, "both" of them should help clean up. Sometimes even this won't work. In the future just restrict what the kids can do or play with and make it clear to the visiting child. Sometimes relatives don't like that, but if they are not going to support what you want in your own house, that's just too bad. Whatever the case, don't take it all out on your child. To be sure, he or she is not an angel but at the same time, the child can't be entirely at fault.

In the end, if your children learn that having a messy room leads to some consequences, it will help you have an easier job of teaching them to keep their things in some kind of order. Remember, they are just little children. Don't expect more from them than they can do and take your time; you have a lot of it.

The third example is the child who throws temper tantrums. Believe me, if the child has had them for a while, this can really be a very difficult situation. The reason that temper tantrums are so difficult is that they are usually reinforced on what is called a variable schedule of reinforcement. A variable schedule of reinforcement is one in which the behavior is not reinforced all of the time. It varies. Sometimes the child is reinforced and sometimes it isn't. It is as if the child learns that if I just do it a little longer or if I throw my fit a few more times, eventually I'll get what I want. In most cases the child wins and gets exactly what he or she wants. Let's change this behavior.

In the beginning, a child throws a fit or cries and we rush to see what is the matter. This is a perfectly normal parental reaction, and it is one we certainly don't want to lose. But the child has learned that when he or she cries you come running. Sometimes a child will cry because he or she wants a snack or in a store the child wants a new toy. Once in a while, we give in and say, "Okay, if you'll just be quiet I'll give you the snack," or, "Okay, okay, you can have the toy; just stop throwing such a fit." Again, this is perfectly normal, and I think, perfectly fine. But, some kids make the connection that, if they cry a little bit they can have what they want. As time goes by the child occasionally has to cry more and more and we give in to it later and later, and as a result, we have helped shape the child's lengthy temper tantrums. Later, when the child wants something we get a full-blown nuclear reaction from him.

How do you stop a temper tantrum? The instructions for stopping it are easy, but putting the instructions into effect are another matter. The real key is consistency. When you say No, you have to stick to your guns. Remember we talked about extinction so that the bell no longer signaled food. No must signal No. If the child has learned that all he or she has to do is stick to it and that you will eventually give in, he or she will stick to it. The longer you wait and then give in the longer you will make the next tantrum. That means that no one gives in, not mom nor dad nor any other relative. This is one place in which you have to ignore the behavior if it is at all possible. If the behavior gets too bad, the behavior should have a consequence. That consequence will have to fit the situation, and you and your mate must agree and stick to it. Believe it or not, the tantrum will eventually go away, but the longer the child has had the tantrum, the longer it will take to go away. But if you stick to it, and I do mean stick to it, your "No means No!"—it becomes an S^D (a cue) for not giving in. Remember, the real key is to teach the child that you are not going to give in because, once you do, you are dead in the water.

The final example that I would like to develop is teaching the child to study. This a difficult one, and I often have college students who still do not have the slightest idea of how to study correctly.

When the child is little we should spend time with him or her, obviously, and some of that time can be spent in learning. You see, studying is learning. If learning from the beginning is associated with time spent with you and you also make it a fun time, then, when the child goes to preschool or kindergarten, he or she will be building off of a firm foundation.

A small digression about preschool. Whether you are using preschool for your child because you are increasing your family income or you are interested in self-enhancement there is strong evidence that the use of preschool does not weaken the mother-child bond. As a result, I have been a strong supporter of a good quality preschool for several reasons and I would like to elaborate on them briefly.

First, when the child is interacting with his or her peers, you will get a chance to see if your child-rearing practices are on track. If you do find something slightly wrong, you will have plenty of time to correct it before the child goes to school or the problem becomes a really serious one. The preschool teacher may also offer some helpful comments. However, before you go all out and take the preschool teacher's comments as the only valid ones, get a second opinion. But do listen. You may learn something that will help your child.

A second reason is that attending preschool provides the child some supervised interaction with his or her age mates. It is a crowded world we live in and the sooner we learn to act and interact with others around us, especially if it is supervised interaction, the better off we are for the experience. So if you have a chance to send your child to a *good* day school or a preschool program, I would strongly recommend it.

While we are still on the topic of using a quality preschool there is one more small digression I would like to make. When your child is away several days a week some parents feel guilty about going out on Saturday night or whenever they would usually go out with their mates.

Remember, you still have a relationship to maintain with your mate. Besides your parent-child relationship you still have a parent-parent or mate-mate relationship. Someday your child will be grown and out of the house. If you let your relationship be only through your child and don't keep the relationship you have with your mate alive and healthy, when your child goes so will your original relationship. In short, keep some balance and work at keeping both parent-child and mate-mate relationships alive and healthy. We, as concerned parents, want the child to have all the help he or she needs to advance his or her clever brain. Without realizing it, parents often make an emotional cripple out of their little genius. A child has an intellectual side and an emotional side. Your child may be a very bright six-year-old, but your child is still a six-year-old emotionally. Develop both sides together and keep both aspects in balance. What good is a great intellect if the person is an emotional cripple? This child will not have a happy life. I am reminded of the little girl in the movie *Parenthood*. If you have seen the movie, you will remember the father who was always drilling his daughter. Do not do this. Fortunately, the father changes and the little girl has a chance to be normal.

Back to studying again. When your child comes home, spend time with the child when he or she studies. Sometimes one parent is a better helper than the other. For example, I don't seem to be a great deal of help to my nine-year-old son when he studies. I love him dearly but we just can't seem to get the job done. My wife, on the other hand, can get him to do almost anything and he seems to love it. When it comes to my next son who is eleven, we can sit down and doing homework with him is a piece of cake. If one parent seems to be better at working with one of the children it is okay to let that parent do the helping. You can work with the other children or you can make supper or do something while they are working on the homework.

Don't spend more than twenty to thirty minutes on homework at any one sitting when the child is in the lower grades. Also, when the children first come home from school, don't make them sit down immediately and do homework. Let them take a break from schoolwork for a while. After they have played for a while, have a regular set time for homework, and go to a place where it is quiet and you won't be interrupted. Watching TV while doing homework is not a good practice to start.

While you are in your home "study" place, do just that and only that, study. If you are going to stop studying, get out of the "study" place. As the years go by, gradually shape children to do homework by themselves, but shape them very gradually.

Always give children your attention when they are showing you their classwork and always reinforce them for good classwork. In this manner they learn that, like their chores around the house, certain things are their responsibility and they will gradually accept these responsibilities over the years and grow into them as if they were a normal part of life. This may seem ridiculously simple, but learning to do your chores around the house and learning that your homework is something that must be done are two of the first steps in shaping the responsible adult. Remember, when a child *earns* things he or she has, whether it is the money for a toy or going to a concert or grades in school, the child will feel better about it and better about himself or herself.

Spend time with children as they start the learning process, don't study too long at any one time, praise them for all of their good works, and shape yourself out of the job. It is all based on the idea that you are going to spend time with your child.

Things to Remember

1. To successfully change a behavior pattern you must:
   A. Determine the target behavior.
   B. Establish the baseline.
   C. Determine the reinforcers.
   D. Use shaping.
2. Always use small steps when introducing a new behavior and be sure your child is successful with these steps.
3. Potty training is a complex process. Go slowly.
4. Assuming responsibilities as a child is the first step toward assuming adult responsibility.

8. Schedules of Reinforcement and Finding Rewards That Work

This is the last chapter in which we attempt to look at some principles of learning. However, this chapter is a logical extension of the reinforcement principles that we have discussed. Even so, after this chapter we shall look at various applications that are very important for parents to know as they attempt to raise their families.

Thus far, we have looked at both positive and negative reinforcement, and I hope that there is no question as to the power of these two principles in determining behavior. But what happens when we take the same behavior pattern and begin to reinforce it in a number of different ways? What if our little boy or girl is showing us some of his or her homework, and we praise the child every single time. With another child, we only occasionally reward him or her for showing us homework. Will this make a difference in the child's behavior? Common sense tells that it will, but let's take a look and see if we can make these schedules work for us.

Why is it that some babies happily go for hours between feedings while others cry for hours? This often has to do with the schedules of reinforcement. The first schedule is called a fixed ratio schedule of reinforcement (FR). In this type of reinforcement schedule, reinforcement is dependent upon the production of a fixed number of correct responses. This means that every time you complete a correct response, you get a reinforcer. The other part of this ratio is that the relationship between the correct responses and a reward remains the same, is fixed.

In some instances the relationship may be one-to-one, whereas at other times the relationship is such that it may take more than one response to obtain a reinforcement. For example, if we praise our child every single time he or she does a correct thing, such as take out the trash or help around the house, we would say that the child was on an FR 1 schedule of reinforcement. We give one reinforcement for each time the child takes out the trash or does something around the house. When children are very little we often utilize an FR 1 schedule without realizing it. At other times there may be a set number of correct responses before we are reinforced. Factory workers doing piecework are paid on an FR schedule. If you must produce a set number of items to make a bonus or to make your "rate," you are being paid on a FR schedule. In other words, the more you do the more you get. As you might suspect, this produces a very high rate of responding. When you work at home you are usually on some type of FR schedule. The more you do the more you get.

The next schedule is called fixed interval schedule of reinforcement (FI). In this schedule it is the interval of time that is fixed, not the number of responses. It is said that in this schedule of reinforcement, reinforcement is dependent upon the production of a single correct response after a fixed interval of time. As an example, let's say that you are sitting in front of a lever, and if you push the lever (correct response), just once at the end of each five-minute period you will receive a piece of candy (reinforcement). While you are waiting for the next five minutes to run out, if you never look at the lever or push it a million times, you would receive nothing. So, it is not just pushing the lever that is important but you must push it at the end of the five-minute time period or nothing will happen, you will receive nothing. As you might suspect, the person or animal in the lab soon learns to do nothing during the time interval but when the time interval is up, the person or lab animal responds. In this example I have used a five-minute interval. Actually, it could be any interval of time varying from a few seconds to a very long period of time. The key is that the time period is fixed and remains the same.

There are many examples of this type of reinforcement in everyday life. If you have your baby on a four-hour feeding schedule and do not vary from that schedule, your child will learn that he will not be fed until the four hours are up. As a result, he will not start to fuss until the time period draws near. He has learned that crying for food during the time period is not reinforced. Of course, as with all children, there may be crying times before the feeding time is up, because children cry for many reasons and not just for food.

The third schedule of reinforcement is the variable ratio schedule of reinforcement (VR). Since it is a ratio schedule, we already know (from the fixed "ratio") that the person will have to perform for reinforcement, and since it is variable, that means that the number of performances will vary. It may vary about a small average number of performances, or it may vary about a large number of performances. We will soon see that this schedule is so powerful that animals in the lab have pushed a lever over 10,000 times for a single reinforcer. Will we humans exhibit similar behavior for a reinforcer? After a little more explanation, we take a look.

In this schedule, reinforcement varies around some average number of performances. In a modern research lab the researcher, using modern electronic equipment, can dial in the number of average performances that is desired. In real life no one is there to dial in the reinforcements, and most reinforcers happen in some random and often unpredictable manner which, as it turns out, is quite like the variable schedule that is set up in the lab.

A person on a VR schedule will produce behavior that is very strong and highly resistant to extinction. The person just won't stop responding. It is as if the animal hasn't learned the difference between extinction and responding just "one more time." For example, a child cries because he or she wants a cookie or a toy. As it turns out that day, maybe the parent has a headache or just doesn't want to listen to the crying so she soothes the child and gives it a cookie. (Remember, whatever behavior leads to a positive reinforcer that behavior increases in frequency.) The next time the child wants something, what behavior has he or she been reinforced for? The child has been reinforced for crying or the beginning of what may become a temper tantrum. So the child cries and we say to ourselves, "Self, I'm not going to give in." If we can hold the line the behavior would disappear, but we don't. Sometimes we give in to it and sometimes we don't. In the process the child learns to cry longer and longer for what it wants. In time *we* have actually created a difficult situation.

We can stop this behavior by holding the line and letting the behavior extinguish. If you go a long time and don't give in, all you have to do is give in one time and you really have caused a problem. Once you decide to stop reinforcing a temper tantrum, you *cannot* give in to the tantrum. Don't let the tantrum have a consequence. As extinction is setting in, you can then reinforce a different behavior pattern.

Another example of a VR schedule is gambling. First, gambling itself must be reinforcing. If it is, it should produce a pattern of behavior that is highly resistant to extinction. And so it is! Gambling pays off in a random fashion. As a result, you are reinforced on a VR schedule. If you pull its handle, the slot machine does not always give you money. Most of the time it doesn't, but once in a while it does. And you are hooked. The same is true of playing poker or betting on the ponies or dogs. It is not easy to beat this type of behavior, and it often takes professional training to work with an individual who has this type of behavior problem. Like many other inappropriate behaviors, you can win only by not participating at all!

Let me give you an experience that I once had with my son when he was about seven years old. We were at a carnival that came to town once a year. Among the many things that the carnival offered was a trailer that was divided by a number of glass partitions. In each partition was a crane that could pick up a prize and deposit it in a chute. The problem was that the crane usually didn't deposit the prize in the chute. It usually fell out of the jaws of the crane before you got it to the chute. Each time you wanted to try again you had to deposit another quarter. Well, my son went through his allowance and all of the extra money that he had brought with him. So he asked for more money and I said, "No." I was not popular with my son or my wife (remember, being a parent is not a popularity contest). He cried and cried and, a few days later, he could not buy what he had been saving his money for. This really made him cry. Despite my loss of popularity as a parent, my son's behavior had a consequence. As a result of that consequence, today my son does not gamble. This is the real lesson that I wanted him to learn.

This brings us to the last schedule of reinforcement, called the variable interval schedule of reinforcement (VI). This schedule also produces a pattern of behavior that is highly resistant to extinction but, as we shall see, in a slightly different manner. The definition of this schedule is that reinforcement is dependent upon the production of a single correct response after a variable interval of time. In English, this means that a person on this type of schedule needs to respond but cannot be sure of exactly when to respond, because the time is always changing. As you might suspect, this schedule produces a great deal of behavior (work) for little reward or reinforcement.

A person who is fishing with a bobber is on a VI schedule. As soon as he gets a bite or catches the fish, he baits the hook and throws it back in and watches the bobber for the next bite. Will a person who is hooked on fishing sit there and wait a long time for the next bite? Yes! Did you ever see a fisherman go home when the fish are biting? No! If the person were fly-fishing, he or she would be on a variable ratio schedule. After how many times of placing the fly on the water will the fish bite? It is going to be some unpredictable number of times. So, this person needs to perform the right response many times. Does a fly fisherman pop that line hundreds of times? You bet. The person with a bobber only needs to perform the correct response once, but after that he or she will wait a long time for the fish to bite so the line can be yanked (correct response). At what time will the fish bite so the bobber will be pulled down? Who knows? That is why it is a VI schedule.

A crucial point that I'm trying to make is that it is the schedule of reinforcement that produces the pattern of behavior. If we are taught some tasks on a low FR schedule, we will extinguish more rapidly for those tasks than if we were taught the same tasks on a VR schedule.

We bring our first child home and we rush to the crib every time the child whimpers. This is placing the child on a small FR schedule. By the time the fourth or fifth child comes home, we certainly don't rush to the crib as quickly or as often as we did for the first one. For the latter child, life starts on a completely different schedule(s) of reinforcement.

If you and your mate go out and come home after a night out and find the baby-sitter tied up in the cellar, you might want to punish the children. We could line them all up and give them a spanking, but wait. If the spanking isn't the thing that affects the behavior of some of the kids it will not have the same effect on all of them. Will it? On top of that, the first one in line is not being reinforced like the last one in line (different schedule), and once again we will have a difference in behavior.

Do you find this confusing? Don't let it be. First, using a learning approach means that we will not produce robots. In order to produce children who are exactly the same, we would need to start with the same genetic structure (which is found only in identical twins) and reinforce the children for exactly the same thing, every single time, all of their lives. This is impossible, so don't worry. Your children won't turn out like carbon copies.

The second point is that when we talk about personality what we are really talking about is the reinforcement history of the child. If the child has stick-to-it-iveness, the child was reinforced on some type of schedule for those behaviors for which it has the stick-to-it-iveness. If an adult gives up on things, then for those things the child was reinforced on some low FR or FI schedule.

With something as simple as a quick glance, we reinforce a whole array of behaviors in each of our children, and from the very first feeding session we start to shape their personalities. It is really in your hands. What do you want to shape? Are there some behaviors that we would want our children to give up easily, whereas there are others that we want them to stick to for a long time? This is one of the decisions you are making as a parent. As we raise our children, this is exactly what we are doing. Pretty heavy responsibility isn't it? It is a job so important that we cannot leave it to be done by someone who is not interested in the development of our children. Nor, is it something we want to leave just to chance. In chapter 10 when we look at love, we continue with this line of reasoning.

I have attempted to show that it is not only what you reinforce your children for, but how you reinforce them that is also important. You might start your child on a low FR schedule when it comes to studying. While your child is in grade school, you sit every night with your child when he or she does homework. As the years go by, you gradually (and I do mean gradually) put your child on a VR or VI schedule and slowly stretch that schedule out farther and farther. You might want to do this for a whole host of behaviors, and I'm sure you can think of some that would be beneficial for the child as an adult.

We have only looked at the four basic reinforcement schedules. Life is more complex than just these four schedules. Often they are hooked together in a host of ways and the reinforcement situation can become very complex. But that is the beauty of living and the joy of raising our children. Some day we can see if what we have planted in them, by means of the various reinforcements, has worked. It is a serious responsibility and one that we want to carefully plan out ahead of time and modify as need be, as time goes by.

Table 8-1 is a brief review of the schedules of reinforcement. After you have read about the four schedules, this table will be a good guide to help refresh your memory.

Table 8-1

Schedules of Reinforcement

Schedule	Definition and Example
Fixed ratio	A fixed correspondence between performance and the reinforcer. (Piecework in a factory.)
Fixed Interval	Requires a single correct response after a fixed period of time. (A baby on a set feeding schedule.)
Variable ratio	A varying relationship between the number of correct performances and the reinforcer. (Gambling or how often we reinforce temper tantrums.)
Variable interval	Requires a single correct response after a varying period of time. (Fishing with a bobber.)

Things to Remember

1. The schedules of reinforcement will produce varying patterns of behavior that we often call "personality."

9. Let's Talk about Sex

Sex can sometimes be a difficult topic for parents and children. We start with the development of sexual identity and the development of a healthy sexual attitude. Toward the end of this chapter we look at a few common sexual problems in childhood that can spill over into adulthood.

In chapters 2 and 3 we talked about classical and operant conditioning, and we return here to these approaches. Research indicates that from the very beginning we treat boys *differently* than we do girls. I will not argue for the right or wrong of these findings except to say that the differential treatment is so. I do not think that this is necessarily harmful, but I think that it has the potential of being harmful when one sex is seen as better than the other. It is okay to be different, but let's not include in that difference the idea of superiority or inferiority.

From the very beginning little girls are treated differently than are little boys. As children grow, the problem with some parents becomes more acute and boys are taught that they are better than little girls or that they don't have to do some of the things that little girls have to do.

Some years ago I was visiting some friends of mine, and after we had talked for a while and some time passed it was time to put their children to bed. They have three children who at that time were eighteen months, three and a half, and five and a half years old. The oldest was a girl and the two youngest were both boys. The mother was going to read a story to them and I asked if I could read the story. My own children were all grown and away at college or in the army so I thought I would enjoy reading to them because I had always enjoyed reading to my own children. Their daughter sat on one leg and the youngest boy sat on the other while the three-and-a-half-year-old boy leaned on the arm of the chair I was sitting in. The three-and-a-half-year-old who was leaning on the arm of the chair had on what I always called footy pajamas. These are the type of pajamas that have feet sewn in them and the pajamas snap together at the tummy and the top shirt of the pajamas snaps up the back. As it turns out the mother had cut the footy part off because the child had outgrown them and there was a strategic hole located in the front of the pants. While I was reading I noticed that the child was using both of his hands to play with his erect penis. I said to myself, "Self, I have a Ph.D. in psychology, I ought to be able to talk the child out of this behavior." I told him how heavy the book we were reading was and after some pleading on my part, he gave up one of his hands to help me hold the book. The other hand was still stimulating his organ (so much for the Ph.D.). Finally, he did give up his other hand and helped me hold the book with both hands. While I was going through this process his mom and dad were sitting on a sofa on the other side of the room. Mom looked like she could crawl under the couch. Dad, on the other hand, looked like he really was proud of this little son and I thought that his chest was going to burst. While mom looked for a place to hide, dad had a proud grin on his face. How often do we praise junior for his equipment or just tell him to "stop doing that"? When it comes to our little "girl" we almost have a fit. I wondered what dad would have done if it had been the little girl playing through the strategic hole and not the little boy. I'll bet his reaction would have been different.

This is one of the important points I want to make in this chapter. We treat boys differently, especially when it comes to sex. We often put a lot of things on the girl that we wouldn't think of putting on the boy. If a boy goes out and seduces every girl in town, many think that he is quite a "man." If the girl seduces the whole football team, what do we think of her? It is clearly not the same thing that we think of the boy. As if that were not bad enough, many parents, because of their own sexual misperceptions or misguided religious convictions, make the girl guilty and a sinner if she shows a normal sexual drive. Now, don't misunderstand me, I am *not* saying that I want young adults going around trying to seduce the world. I *do not!* What I want is for them to learn to respect their bodies and to develop a healthy sexual outlook. I want both the males and females to be treated in an equal and healthy manner.

Those of you who already have children may remember when your child discovered his or her hand. As they watch their hand move they gradually begin to learn that this is a part of them and they are controlling the movements. If you have ever experienced this as a parent, it is one of those milestones in development that you always remember. This is not different from a child discovering any other part of his or her body, but if it is the genital area we often *overreact*. When we do, we may be associating a negative or fearful emotion with this area of the body.

In chapter 4 we looked at the sympathetic and parasympathetic parts of the nervous system. The sympathetic division is associated with arousal or, more commonly, fight or flight, and the parasympathetic division is associated with a relaxed state. In order to understand some of the problems that parents cause, we need to investigate this nervous system a bit further.

When we say that the sympathetic division is associated with arousal or fight or flight, that arousal is *not* sexual arousal. If we examine the development of the human species this actually makes sense. Picture a human male in very ancient times, a time before Levi jeans, a comfortable old shirt, and your favorite pair of sneakers. We are out in the wilderness clad only with body hair and perspiration (this is even before deodorant). We might be armed with a club or a rock. If we are attacked by a saber-toothed tiger, what is the last thing we would need? That's right, an erection. What would the fellow have done with it? In fact, the saber-toothed tiger might have removed it! So when we were developing into modern man the sympathetic nervous system was used to marshall all of the bodily forces for survival. Blood is pumped to the muscles, our senses are sharper, adrenalin is pouring into the system, digestion is halted, and we are literally ready for fight or flight (the second part of this has always been more appealing to me). When the danger has passed, our body cannot maintain this pace so we need to reverse the effects of the sympathetic nervous system. This is where the parasympathetic nervous system comes into play. It reverses or slows down those functions that have been utilized for the fight-or-flight responses. And it is the parasympathetic division that is associated with "sexual arousal." In the wild, relaxed and out of danger, the man, as well as the woman, can turn his or her thoughts to other things (e.g., the birds and the bees). To this day, because of the nervous system that we have inherited from ancient man in the wild, the same nervous system is still working in us.

Why have I made such a point of this? If a young man or young lady is frightened or nervous about sexual matters because of what he or she has learned as a child, what will happen when it is appropriate for sexual behavior to take place? The answer to this question is that nothing will happen and that is the problem. This can be avoided if we as parents will take the right approach to sexual matters. After all, we want our kids to enjoy sex as adults, to share it as a gift with that person they will have as their mate, and when the behavior is appropriate. The problem is that as parents we often get appropriate and inappropriate sexual behavior mixed up. And instead of teaching them that sex is a normal and healthy response when it's appropriate, we teach them how never to be able to engage in a beautiful shared physical relationship with their mate. Here is how you can avoid teaching the wrong thing.

First, when your little boy discovers his penis or your little girl her vagina, don't make it a fearful event. After your children have explored this fascinating part of their body don't make it a major crime. Let them explore it for a while. Then change the subject or get the child to do something else. *Do not* scream and holler and/or hit your child for doing this exploratory behavior. If you do, from the very beginning the genital area will become associated by the child with this emotion. In short, via classical conditioning we associate the sympathetic nervous system (this is the nervous system that is concerned with "fight or flight" and not sexual behavior) with the genital area. If you keep building on this your child, as an adult, will not be able to enjoy the joys of a shared physical and emotional sexual relationship. Surely, you want to give your child a chance as an adult. Relax. As the child gets older we need to tell him or her that there are times when we do not exhibit certain behaviors in public. You can teach the child how to act appropriately without making the child a sexual cripple as an adult.

Another thing you should do is to answer children's questions as honestly as you can at a level that they can understand for their age. You don't need to go into graphic detail, but you should answer sexual questions in a straightforward manner. I once knew a lady who told her children that babies came from their "belly button." This has given me a few laughs, but I wonder what her children thought when they found that this was not true. There are times when some of their questions will really make you think, but I am convinced that an honest answer, one they can understand at their level, is the best thing for their later adult sexual development.

What kind of questions do children ask? All kinds. For example: they will ask where babies come from, and little boys and girls will ask why a boy's penis gets erect. As they get older they will continue to ask more and more difficult questions.

Once when my oldest son was about eight years old, a TV commercial advertised a feminine hygiene solution that the announcer said "was to be taken internally." My son asked me, "Do you drink it?" He really caught me off guard. I said, "Your mom will explain it!" We still kid about that one. My wife said, "Okay, Mr. Psychologist, you explain it!" Hopefully, you will do better at explanations then I did. You are going to be caught in some difficult questions and sometimes you will be at a loss for words, but you should *try* to answer each question honestly and at a level the child can understand.

One more tale that will show how a confusion that developed during childhood can be carried into adulthood and cause a problem. A woman in therapy once told me that she couldn't believe that she was pregnant with her sixth child because she couldn't ever remember having an orgasm. That isn't exactly how she put it, but I couldn't believe her level of understanding for a thirty-five-year-old woman. Needless to say, I gave her a crash course in the reproductive process. And do you know what happened? She didn't believe me; she really didn't believe me. You do not want to send your children into adulthood with such sexual misconceptions.

The real challenge is to teach children to respect themselves and still give them the gift of having the ability to have a healthy relationship with their mates. First of all, if we don't have a healthy sexual relationship it is going to be hard to teach it to our children. If you feel your sexual relationship is far from perfect, seek professional help. We know so much more today about human and psychological functioning. If you break a bone, the magic of the body mends it all by itself, but if something is wrong with your personality or some aspect of it, it will almost always get worse unless you get off of your duff and do something about it. So for you and potentially for your child, if this is a problem area, get help. You don't want your child to go through all the misery that you have experienced. So do it. If you need help go get it.

When you seek professional help, try to find a psychologist who has graduated from an accredited program that is recognized by the American Psychological Association. It is your life or that of your child you are dealing with, and it will also affect the life of your mate. Don't be afraid to ask for the person's credentials.

It is often difficult to get a man to therapy, especially if he has a sexual problem. Somehow we have taught males in our culture that this is some sign of weakness or, if we males have a sexual problem, it's really the "woman's problem," not ours. That's just baloney. Sometimes in the process of growing up, because of well-meaning but misguided parents, a lesson was taught to us that led us down a road to sexual "un"enjoyment. Fortunately, we humans have a fantastic talent. We can unlearn inappropriate behavior and learn appropriate behavior. With a little professional help you and your mate can get rid of your hangups and learn a new way to act and interact with each other. There is only one catch. You have to do something about it. So if you need to, do it!

As a parent, one of the times that becomes difficult to deal with sex is during and after your child's puberty. This can be a scary time for the child and the parent, especially if the parent and child are already on shaky ground sexually. Again, if the child has a question, answer it in words he or she can understand. If you don't know the answer, there are plenty of books in the library or a reputable bookstore that can help you solve the mystery. But, keep the communication lines open. Don't criticize the child for asking the question. Do you remember some of the questions that you had at that age? I can still remember many of the questions that I had that were very confusing to me, especially when young adolescents got together. Boy, did we come up with some kooky answers!

The other part of this communication process is that you shouldn't make healthy sex "dirty" or somehow "sinful." Again, answer the questions but also try to get your children to see that the gift of their love is one of the most precious things that they have. They should not throw it away. Think of the diseases that could be controlled in this manner or the unwanted pregnancies that could be avoided.

The discussion of sexual behavior can be a most difficult area, but without sex none of us would even be here. Remember, keep the parasympathetic division (this is the part of the nervous system that is associated with a relaxed state) plugged in so that the child will someday have a chance to share a most precious gift with the person who will become his or her mate for life. If you had a choice to give this gift of sharing to your child, wouldn't you give it? You can. Whatever gift the child shares you have had a part in it.

Things to Remember

1. Children are curious and will ask many questions. Some of these questions will also include questions on sex. Answer them honestly and in simple terms.
2. Don't associate the sympathetic nervous system with sex. If this is done to an extreme, you may inhibit your child's adult sexual behavior.
3. You serve as a role model for your children. If you are having a problem with some area of sex don't pass it on to your children. Seek help.

10. Learning How to Share Love

I have often thought that one of the core problems with loving is that from the time our children are very small we don't teach them the right lesson and approach to love. When we were little and mom or dad read fairy tales or stories to us, almost all of the endings went, ". . . and they lived happily ever after." Remember what we said about all of the things that are being associated at this time by means of classical and operant conditioning, the association of your parasympathetic nervous system, and all of the things that are associated with that time and space. Along with this whole package, our close association with mom or dad, the good feelings, comes a myth. This myth sounds great and makes wonderful endings to stories or fairy tales, but it doesn't match reality. In fact, I think that it can actually hinder effective loving because it teaches us that love requires no work. It just happens by magic, and if it doesn't, it isn't "really" love.

Nowhere do we tell our kids about the amount of good, hard work and compromise that go into making a family unit and a love relationship work. So when things get a little stormy, I think that we are actually teaching kids that life is a lot like watching television. If we don't like the program, we can simply change channels. If the marriage isn't working, we can simply change mates and with no-fault divorce it is about as easy as changing channels with a remote control. You hardly have to do much more than move a finger and bingo, before you know it, it's done. Now you are ready to find that "real" love, the one that happens like magic. You know, "one puff from your burning heart and it's springtime."

There are a number of lessons in the previous statements. The first is, if you can make a marriage work, stay in it and make it work. Divorce is tough on everyone and you pay for it a long time after the legal work is complete. This is especially true for the kids. The lawyers for the parents see to it that everything is divided up, but no lawyer represents the kids. Both you and your "ex" have a lawyer, but the wishes of the kids often go out the window and it is they who truly pay for the divorce. There are some emotional scars that take a long time to heal, so that for some kids, along with all the difficulty of growing up today, the scars from divorce don't ever seem to heal. (For example, children often incorrectly believe they were the cause of the divorce.)

However, there are times when two people have grown so far apart that staying together is pure hell or one of the partners is so physically or psychologically abused that staying together is not only impossible but it isn't healthy either. I am convinced that there are times when a divorce can be a viable option; not a first option, but a viable option. Just be sure to remember that you haven't gotten a divorce from your responsibilities as a parent. Those responsibilities never stop, divorce or no divorce.

We continue some of this line of thought in chapter 11 when we look at making a blended family work, but for now let's get back to learning how to love. As I stated in the beginning, we don't teach our kids the right lesson about loving. Since we've been little, we have heard from our parents or our teachers in school time and time again, "If you want to be good at something you must practice,

practice, practice." We practice how to walk, to run, to ride a bike, to say the alphabet, to do math, to play an instrument, or to do whatever it is that we want to do well. It's practice, practice, practice! And sure enough, after a while we get better at what we've been practicing. Orel Hershiser wasn't born knowing how to pitch. He developed that skill after many, many years of, you guessed it, practice.

So, where and how did we learn to love? I don't mean the learning of sexual positions but learning how to love and share and give of yourself and make a marriage relationship work. Where is the book on this? Where in grade school or high school did you learn to do this? What we learned was, once married, happy or not, you were in a lifelong relationship, or for some a prison that you weren't supposed to get out of. But, how do you make it an enjoyable experience, an experience that we want to last a whole lifetime? Well, you aren't going to learn it all in this chapter but perhaps I can give you a few things to think about so that you can make a love relationship work and in the process, hopefully, teach your children how to travel through life with the skills needed for making a happy and loving relationship work. Herein lies the fallacy of the fairy tales. Making a relationship enjoyable and keeping it alive and growing are skills, and you have to practice these skills to be good at them. You do not just live happily ever after. The problem is, we really aren't set up to teach our children these skills because most parents don't know the necessary components of the skills to be able to teach them. So, how can we teach someone to practice something we don't even know ourselves?

Consider the following eight points and after you have read this chapter and some time has passed, give yourself a test and see if you are following some of these points and making your relationship with your mate grow and become enjoyable. I'm not doing this just for you. This entire book is really aimed at trying to show you how to raise happy and psychologically healthy kids. But some of it has to start with you as a parent. If you practice this, it will be easier for them to see what you are doing and it will also make it easier for you to talk to them about how to love someone. You will be teaching them by example so they can take advantage of imitation learning and you will also be teaching by your verbal instructions so they can begin to make that learning part of their very being.

I should like to make two brief points before we begin. First, the following eight points are in no special order. They are so interrelated that no one point is more important than the other. Also, the list of points is clearly not exhaustive. There are certainly many other points, but these few will at least give you a starting point.

Second, I want to make a brief statement about imitation learning. We have briefly mentioned imitation learning before, but I would like to stress the importance of this type of learning. Much of what we learn is by imitation, that is, observing another and then trying to duplicate his/her behavior. We imitate famous sports stars (why do you think famous stars advertise products?), and a host of popular or important people as well as our mom or dad. We each have a favorite hero whom we often imitate. Think of the many skills that you know, and if you go back into your memory you will discover that many of these skills were learned from observing and imitating others. This is especially true of our parents. Think of the things that we have observed our parents doing and later imitated. There isn't anything wrong with this, but what I want to stress is its importance and power in shaping human behavior. Let me offer the following example to demonstrate the importance of imitation or observational learning and I think that you will see how necessary it is that you provide the correct example to be observed and imitated.

Research indicates that many parents who abuse their children were themselves abused children. At first thought this doesn't make sense; at least it didn't to me. If you experienced an abusive childhood, why would you want your own flesh and blood to experience that same horror? Somehow in my gut that still doesn't make sense. Unfortunately, in terms of learning, it makes all too much sense. When a person has been abused as a child, this is also the behavior that he or she observed. As a result, the model of behavior that the person learned is one of abuse. Obviously, I do not want you to abuse your children. I want you, as a parent, to provide a healthy model to your children, so they will know how to share love, not abuse. That is why I have often stated, if there is a problem go and get some professional help.

If you have no idea how to love in a healthy and growing way, how can you teach it to your kids? Let's give the kids a chance to enjoy a fulfilling life and relationship. So, if some of these eight points apply to you, practice them so that both you and your children can begin to learn to practice the skill of sharing love. With a little practice you can develop this skill, like you would develop any skill with practice, and you and your children will not live in a dead end fairy tale of ". . . they lived happily ever after." Instead, it will read ". . . because they worked at sharing love, they lived happily ever after."

Love lesson 1. Be yourself and don't play games.
If you start a relationship by being yourself, then you do not have to change character somewhere down the

line. I'm not saying that we shouldn't put our best foot forward when we meet people, but we must live within our true personality. Don't say you like something, or that you are going to do something, and then do otherwise. In the end, you'll become alienated from your true self, and the bigger the gulf between your true self and the role you are playing, the more problems you will have and the more "unhappy" you will be. This certainly isn't a new idea in psychology as Carl Rogers pointed out many years ago, but it is an idea that has application in this setting. You can't be happy in the long run and play games with what you like or who you are.

Certainly, be kind to those around you and treat others the way you would like to be treated (another old idea) but don't create an unrealistic world and then try to live in that unrealistic world. It won't work. Don't do it and don't try to teach your kids to do it. Your children see you at home in a way that others do not see you. If you try to create an unrealistic world for whatever reason, you won't be happy and, more than that, you are not modeling a behavior that will help your children make a healthy adjustment to life.

I keep saying "a growing relationship" and I think that it would be fitting to make a small digression and explain what I mean about a growing relationship. A growing relationship is one in which you and your mate have the psychological space to develop into individuals who maximize their potential without the other person detracting from that potential. It is one in which you continue to appreciate that individual such that you both desire to continue the relationship as one of the most important events in your life. It is a shared growth, a process that is continually in flux around a core of both individual and common growth. It is a continuing dynamic process, not a goal that is reached and forgotten.

You cannot grow in a relationship if you grow toward a false state or process. Teach your children to say what they feel and to get in touch with their feelings. You can go a long way in doing this by having the children make "I" statements, such as "I feel," "I like," "I need," and so on. This doesn't mean that we let children be rude or scream their wants and desires. I think that this process can be accomplished within a civil and respectful relationship. You can be in touch with your true identity and begin to learn to accept and like it without being a cruel or disrespectful person. In the process of respecting ourselves, we must also learn to respect those around us. These are two separate things to learn. They are often confused as one single learning event so that if you have one, you automatically have the other. Not so. We must learn the two separate lessons.

In short, when you are in a relationship, be honest with yourself as well as the other individual. If the children see you doing this, you will be setting a good example that will lead to your happiness and one for them to imitate. Remember, your interaction with the child produces a child who is capable of love; this is done when children can observe your examples of hugging, praising, and playing with them.

Love lesson 2. Be friends.

When you are young and in love, it is hard to imagine that you won't spend much of your life in bed. We often spend so much time worrying about who we love and how good are we at making love that we forget, at least in the beginning, that there is a difference between loving someone and liking someone. In the end, I have found that many couples whom I have counseled loved each other very much, but they never really liked each other.

In our culture today, we live in a time in which we do not delay our gratification. If I want something, I want it right now. Why wait? The same is true of relationships. Why not enjoy all of the joys of a relationship? Why wait? In the process, we become so involved with love and the process of falling in love that we forget that we also need to be friends with this person. When you are not in bed and the kids are gone, what are you going to do? Do you know what your mate likes or dislikes? Do you share common friends or activities or hobbies? Certainly we don't want the two of you to be carbon copies of each other; that would be very dull and boring. But what common ground do you have? This may seem a little old-fashioned, but that was what "old-fashioned" courting and dating were all about. A lasting relationship, like that great oak, takes time to develop. Today's young lovers are so busy practicing for the honeymoon that they don't give the real honeymoon a chance to take place and develop into a "honeymoon for life." Friendships usually last a lifetime. Please teach your children also to be a friend to the person they love. If you are willing to do this, they have an excellent example to follow, and both of you will have a better chance at a long-lasting and happy relationship. Friends usually do things for each other and don't think about it. Are you friends with your life's partner and are you teaching your children to do the same? For that matter, are you friends with your kids?

For example, do you spend time and do things with your children just for the sheer delight of doing it? When you go somewhere, do you invite the children to come with you as you would invite a friend to come along with you just to share his or her company? These are but a few examples, but I think you can get the idea of what I want you to try.

Love lesson 3. Talk in bed.

Obviously talking is not one of the first things that you think of when you go to bed and yet, it can be more important than the other thing you think of as *the* bedtime activity.

This may seem far removed from raising kids or even having any, but it is very important. When the day is finished and you are with your mate, do you share what happened to you during your day? Do you tell him or her what you like or dislike? Or do you tell your secretary or friend at work? If you do, you are not growing with your mate but you are growing with someone else. You can't blame your mate for not understanding you if you won't tell him or her how you feel or what's important.

Now, I'm not saying that you should not have other confidential relationships. They can have a place in your life, but if you are going to continue to share a growing relationship, you must keep talking and communicating and listening. Don't just go to bed and satisfy your physical needs and then fall asleep. You will end up falling out of a relationship. When was the last time the kids heard you laughing in your bedroom or just lying there talking? Honest, open communication is the fertile soil within which love continues to grow and thrive. Again, what do you want to teach your kids? So talk and share your victories and defeats with your love, and I promise you that you will have a relationship that others will envy, and one that will be satisfying and fulfilling for you.

Love lesson 4. Touch your mate.

As you pass your wife or husband during the day, do you reach out and touch each other? Do you show your affection openly to your mate?

You can live in an emotional suit of armor and you won't get hurt, but it sure isn't any fun. What will it cost to reach out and touch each other's hand, or kiss each other's cheek as you pass each other during the day? When was the last time that you patted your lover as you passed him or her or squeezed his or her hand or said "I love you," or kissed and hugged? Now, I'm not saying you ought to get sloppy about it and seduce each other on the floor in front of the kids. We only go through life one time, why not share as much of the relationship as you can?

If we show our love for each other openly and honestly, we will have children who will seek to do the same thing in their lives and with the person they have selected as their mate. What have you got to lose? Actually nothing, and you have so much to gain, a happier life for you and the potential of a happier life for your children. What a legacy to leave to your children and your grandchildren. So touch. The more you touch, the less chance that love will break.

Love lesson 5. Put your mate first.

This is really a very simple and old idea, but I think that it is very important in developing a richer relationship for yourself, and it is a terrific example to set for the kids. For some time the idea that "I'm not responsible for your happiness" or "I'm not responsible for your problems" has done a disservice to people attempting to develop a strong caring relationship. With that attitude you are less likely to get hurt, but you are also less likely to develop a relationship with a caring person. It is true that we must care for ourselves and that this in turn helps us to care about others, but it would be a shallow world of relationships if all we ever did was just to look after ourselves. When you do something, think about your mate. Would he or she like it or be happy about what you are saying or doing? Again, we can't get completely lost in another person. This isn't healthy either. If you wanted that, you might as well marry a mirror and then you would get the perfect narcissistic reflection of yourself. However, this wouldn't be very much fun on long winter nights.

Think of your mate. If you do something for your mate, it doesn't mean that you are his or her slave. It means that you love that person and you are not afraid of showing it. Just think how nice it might be if in relationships people enjoyed doing things for others. Remember when I said that there aren't specific boy or girl jobs around the house, just work that needs to be done? When was the last time you helped around the house or took the time to work in the yard or on the car together? I'm not trying to be critical, but do things for each other and you will have pleasant things done tó and for you. Again, what a lesson to show the children. As we give of ourselves, so shall we receive more in return. Give it a try, and you will be surprised how much you will actually be doing for your children and for yourself. If children learn by example, can you imagine what your home will be like?

Love lesson 6. Do things together and separately.

It is true that I asked you to share more of yourselves and to do things together. At the same time if that was all you ever did your relationship wouldn't have much vitality. It is like saying if two aspirins take away my headache, the whole bottle would make me feel terrific. Nonsense.

So it is with a relationship. There are times when we need to get out and do things on our own. It can keep vitality in your relationship and it will give you something to talk about when the two of you go to bed. If it's a ladies night out for cards or some of the fellows are going to a baseball game or hunting, that can be a healthy thing for your relationship. Again, it teaches the children to have balance in their relationship(s) when they get older. Just remember, these times are for adding some change in what we do that will strengthen the relationship, not weaken it. After all, some absence does make the heart grow fonder.

Love lesson 7. Accept the person for who he or she is and don't try to change him or her.

It is one thing for two people to grow together over time, but it is another thing for you to *remake* your mate. In a sharing relationship we all learn to give and take, but that isn't what I mean by this point. If your mate has a particular behavior pattern that is a part of that person, don't feel that your life's goal is to change it. Certainly we change over time, but there is usually a core that is us even with the changes over time. If you are so determined to change that core, why did you marry that person to begin with? This type of thing usually drives two people further apart, not closer together. There is only so much you can give and change and still be you. Again, this is what dating is all about. Can this be the person you would be willing to "share" your life with? So take the time to see if this is the person for you, your friend and mate for life.

It can be a very difficult thing to decide where one's core ends and acceptable change for your mate begins. This is something that takes time and sometimes a bit of argument. Sometimes a good, healthy argument isn't all bad. It can clear the air and will let you know where you and your mate stand on issues. As I've stated before, you don't want carbon copies in a marriage relationship or when raising children. Usually it takes a few years of marriage to arrive at a comfortable balance as far as your core personality and what you are willing to change for your mate. Just give it time and don't rush it. It really does come with time. But if you make him or her over too much you will lose the very person you fell in love with. In the end, for all of your gain you will be a loser.

Love lesson 8. Don't keep score.

An important thing to remember is not to keep score in terms of who does what. If you have followed the previous points there is no reason to keep score. If you put your mate first and your family relationship first, keeping score loses meaning. Maybe this week you made supper more than you usually do, or took the kids somewhere when it wasn't your turn. In the long run it will be fine. But if you keep a score pad handy in your pocket (or head) and keep throwing it up to your mate, the two of you will grow to resent each other. There are times when we only give 10 percent in a relationship and there are other times when we give 190 percent; but, in the long run if the two of you "work together" for the relationship as a whole, the relationship will grow and you will benefit from it. Ask yourself, "Self, what is more important, keeping score or being happy?" So give it a chance and it will grow and be rewarding to you beyond your wildest dreams. When you look at the alternatives, what have you got to lose? As with the children when they are small, this relationship and its success are in your hands. Go for it!

I have spent some pages on what initially looks like material meant only for adults. Remember, I'm trying to help you raise your children. If you don't know what to do in your own life, how can you show the children what to do? Try these "love lessons" and you will have much more to offer the children. They will not only live in a happier home, but you will give them some models to imitate that will help ensure a happier life for them. What an inheritance!

Things to Remember

1. Be yourself and don't play games.
2. Be friends.
3. Talk in bed.
4. Touch your mate.
5. Put your mate first.
6. Do things together and separately.
7. Accept your mate for who he or she is and don't try to change him or her.
8. Don't keep score.

11. The Blended Family or Are All These Kids Ours?

A blended family is a family that is a "blend" of two or more other families. That is, it is a family in which a mother brings her children or a father brings his children into a new family relationship or one of the new parents may come without any children. It is not an original blood family. This chapter is designed to help you adjust to your new family so that you can begin to have the type of married life that you have always wanted. After a brief introduction about second marriages in general, I zero in on the children of a blended family, from the "new father's" and then the "new mother's" view point. This chapter, however, like most other things in life, can never answer all of the questions that are asked. Human life is much too complex. Hopefully, you will get some ideas that you can apply to your unique situation, and will help you and your new mate get started in the direction of a satisfying life so that you can help the children through this difficult adjustment period.

Some of you who read this chapter may be widowed and may be contemplating the upcoming marriage and new family. Statistics, however, appear to indicate that most of you will be divorced. Whether you are widowed or divorced, you will find the information contained in this chapter helpful in your adjustment process.

I include this chapter for two basic reasons. First, as a psychologist and as a student of human behavior, I felt that I might be able to offer some help to the thousands of people who are attempting to blend together two different families. Second, about a decade ago and after sixteen years of marriage, I found myself going through a divorce. In 1985, I married a lovely lady who had three children. At the time of our marriage her children were four, six, and eight years of age. At that time my children, by my first marriage, were sixteen, eighteen, and twenty years of age. My two daughters were living with their mother and my son who was eighteen was in the army. Since that time my son finished his tour of duty in the army and is living with my new wife and me while he is going to college. As I write this the children who are living with us are nine, eleven, thirteen, and twenty-three years of age. On top of that, my wife is Protestant and I am Catholic.

Obviously, my wife and I have had to do some adjusting. Perhaps not as much as some of you who are reading this, but enough, and coupled with my experience and training as a psychologist, I could, I hope, make a few suggestions that might guide you through some difficult times that are ahead. Whenever you get different people in one house with different values and different discipline systems and you are trying to make something work, there are some difficult moments even under the best of conditions and intentions.

Don't despair, it can be worked out if you want it to be, but it doesn't happen by magic. It takes some long days, a lot of work, and a great, great deal of love and understanding. On top of that throw in an "ex" who doesn't always cooperate with what you are trying to do and there are days when you want to throw in the towel. But, with some work and time, you can make it into that ideal marriage and shared love that you always thought there should be.

One of the other obstacles is that once you get a divorce and things start to go bad, you end up in a mind-set of thinking about another divorce. It solved the problem last time, why not try the solution that worked before? Again, you can make it work, but—let there be no mistake about it—it takes a lot of work and patience.

After the dust has settled from a divorce, one of the best things you can do for yourself and your children is to spend some time alone and some quality time with your own children. Being alone lets you settle your anger, your disappointment, and some of the things on your mind, and it allows time for you to examine your mistakes so you can work on them. If you don't, you will carry the same personality traits and bad habits into a new marriage that didn't work in a previous marriage. Why doom your new relationship to failure? It doesn't make sense, so don't do it! Believe it or not, even though your contributions to the divorce may have been small ones, you still made some. Spending time alone lets you sort out your thinking and begin to practice new behaviors and new thinking that will give your new relationship a fighting chance. Without this "time out," you fall back into the same old habits and, bingo, another failure. If some time has passed and you still feel there are leftover problems from your marriage or divorce, remember, seek some professional help. It is a wise thing to do.

If you start dating or get married right away, you can hide some of the contributions you made in the original marriage and resulting divorce. I think this is especially dangerous when sex is involved. By the time a divorce takes place you probably haven't had much sex for a while and without realizing it you begin to let sex sway your thinking. You say to yourself, "Self, I've finally found a guy [or gal] who likes sex as much as I do and in the way that I do. Man, this must be real love." Well, the sex may be wonderful, but I think that it is often masquerading as love. I'm not saying that you shouldn't enjoy it. But I don't think that it is really love, at least not very often. You are just as vulnerable and subject to infatuation as you were the first time around.

We return to the subject of getting married too soon. You can get caught up in the dating, sex, relatives, your prospective new mate's friends, the new kids and on and on. All of these things may be sweeping us into a new marriage; however, some of the problems that caused you to get a divorce are still there just waiting to ambush your new relationship. "See," we tell ourselves, "it was all my 'ex's' fault," and we can be great at hiding from all of *our* contributions that caused the original divorce. We project the marriage failure and usually everything else that has happened wrongly in the Western world onto our ex. However we do it, in the end, we must come to terms with our contributions and make the appropriate mental and behavioral changes. Remember, what we want is success, not another failure.

Before we actually begin looking at the kids and how to help them and you adjust to this new family, there is one promise I'd like you and your new mate to make to each other. It is a very simple thing. Keep open a verbal line of communication. What I want you to do is talk to each other and listen, really listen, to each other. I don't mean with sex; I mean with words. The minute something happens that bothers you, you must get it out in the open. However, I don't mean that you start screaming without regard for each other's feelings. I mean that you should sit down in private and put all of your cards on the table.

Don't put your mate on the defensive. Disagree constructively! Before we can do anything else, that has to come first. If there was ever a list of marriage commandments one of the first commandments of marriage would be: the family that talks together stays together.

If you think about it a minute, it makes sense. Often in the "old marriage," what began to happen over time? We stopped communicating. We can probably think of a dozen reasons why it happened, but the unfortunate thing is that it did happen. Let's not relive that whole scene again. If from the very beginning we have open and honest communication in our marriage, we will start a very healthy habit and be on the right track. Despite what we might think, our mates are not mind readers and "love" all by itself doesn't take you automatically into the thoughts of your lover (another part of the myth that we discussed in chapter 10). This is one of the myths about love and marriage that we want to correct from day one.

Is something bothering you? Fine, get together with your mate and get it out into the open. We don't want to hurt him or her, but as time goes by and these little things continue to build and get away out of proportion, before we know it the relationship is on its way to another divorce. So, what have you gained? Decide which will hurt more. Get the things that are bugging you out in the open. If we lift a few pounds at a time, in time, we can lift a lot of weight. The same is true of our psyche or mind, or our feelings. Little problems that are taken care of as they arise can be handled easily, but, if we let them build we can't handle them. Not only can't we handle them, but often there is some nuclear psychic explosion in which even the rational become irrational, and everything is blown so out of proportion that we wouldn't know an objective point of view if it came up and bit us, even if it bit us in a sensitive spot.

There is another part of this that is assumed but often not stated. That is, when you and your "main squeeze" decide on something or some course of action that means that you stick with it. If something is bothering you about how things are going, talk it over with your mate, not some friend or another lover who "really, really understands you." Remember, you *can* make this work. Yes, it is going to take some labor but it will work, and in the process you will be learning what you can do to ensure that it does work.

Well, enough of this subject. These are some of the things that I have often said to individuals who are looking to take that second or even third plunge. Let's look at the guys first.

So, you've come as a knight on a white charger and you're going to sweep her off her feet and save her. Her "ex" wasn't nice to her, didn't really appreciate her and love her (at least not the way you do), and her savior has finally come.

That is a myth.

It probably always has been and probably always will be. Don't get excited. You can be her knight in shining armor, but the picture isn't that easy to paint. Let's take it a small step at a time so that when we are finished you will have a better appreciation of what has happened and what is likely to happen. Then you will have a better appreciation of what is involved, and a much better chance of being in the same house together after the first two difficult years have passed.

As I stated in the beginning of this chapter, most of the men reading this book have been through a divorce and in some cases two or more divorces. Before you enter another situation and fail, it might be instructive to run a few things through your mind. Have you sat down, when no one is around, and listed some of the reasons you or your former mate wanted the divorce? Let's look at some of them, again, from a guy's point of view.

First, "she spent too much money." Some of the men I have worked with placed this complaint at the top of their list. "I work harder than anyone else I know. I have two jobs and I have less than anyone I know and it's all because she spends too much." I have heard this phrase so often it almost sounds like a broken record. We are going to review a few such scripts and see if we can find the hidden errors with the thinking that is involved.

An obvious problem with this scenario is that the guy is overusing the defense mechanism of projection. Projection is when we "project" (hence the name) our difficulties on to someone else. There isn't really anything wrong with this mechanism. We all use it, but when we overuse it so that the false reality we've created becomes our only reality, we are getting off the mark. All of the problems you experienced weren't just her fault. You played a part too. As males, because we "work," we often don't want to consider all of the money we spend. After all, we *are* working and aren't we entitled to these things because we "work?" If we look at the cost of that new car or pickup truck or time spent in the tavern, or the cost of some of our toys and the fun trips that we had to have, we can see that these things cost a lot and certainly didn't help our finances. "But I work," we tell ourselves. But we need to be more critical of the spending that we did also. Perhaps not always but too often if we are more objective we will find that, even though "we work," we also spend. It was not all "her" fault.

Another common theme that I often hear is that the fellow feels that he was married to "sister superior." "She doesn't like sex, doesn't do it (at least not very often), and when she does, she acts like she is doing me a favor." Does any of this sound familiar?

Many of us who have been divorced stopped communicating (talking) and growing with our former mate. Remember, you need the parasympathetic nervous system engaged for sexual behavior to occur. When we don't keep our lines of communication open with our mate, how can sexual activity take place? In your former marriage, when was the last time you set aside some time for healthy and creative energetic sex? Or was sex something you did just before you fell asleep when you were tired, or really didn't put your heart into what you were doing? I'll bet that with your new mate you are not just doing it when you are dog tired, or because you have to. Let's keep it vital. Stop a minute and examine your new sex life. I'll bet the two of you talk and touch and spend time before and after sex. Keep it that way and it will continue to be rewarding.

I haven't gone this far afield just to talk about sex. If you are working hard at being "happy" you will be a lot more pleasant with the children and that is what I really am aiming at. So, take a little time with your mate and be creative. Bring her a flower or a gift and remind her that she is your main and only "squeeze." You will look forward to coming home, and your new wife and children will look forward to it as well.

We could go on looking at a few more examples but I think the point I'm trying to get across would be the same. This is a new situation. Don't bring along with you the old solutions that didn't work before. Don't act or react with your new mate the way you did with your old one. Don't repeat the old mistakes. Look at what you did that was wrong and correct it. Work every day at making your life and love vital and keep it new. You can only do this by *working* at it. Remember it doesn't happen by itself as it does in a fairy tale or in the movies.

For the gals, there have also been a number of common complaints. Some of the complaints have been the same that the guys are complaining about, so let's look at these same complaints from the female point of view.

"He thinks that I spend too much. But he doesn't sit down with me and pay the bills or go with me to the store and buy groceries or clothes for the kids. If he did, he would see that I am working to stretch what we have to make it go as far as I can."

Does any of this sound familiar? If you are like some of the couples that I've talked to, I'm sure it does. Or how about, "He lies on the couch all evening or weekend, doesn't take a bath, never talks to me and then, when he starts drinking, he wants to make love. And he tells his friends that I'm 'sister superior.' Forget him!"? At this point the wife often reminds the husband that he can go where it's quite warm and he can take along his own ice water.

I have zeroed in on these two examples to demonstrate several points. I am not trying to side with the husband or wife in these examples, and from both sides the examples appear to have some merit. The whole point is that in most of these kinds of cases the people have stopped talking. They are talking to others instead of each other, and they have quit working on their relationship. Is this a good example to show the kids? No! Is this a good way to make a new relationship work? No! Remember, I want you to *work together* to produce happy and healthy children. You can't do it if you are acting like the couples did in the brief examples given.

Now, let's consider the kids in a blended family. For his or her kids you were not there to do all of the childhood bonding that we discussed in earlier chapters. If that's not bad enough, most of the time when an individual embarks on that second venture, the kids are too old to breast- or bottle-feed so don't try it. That early bonding is lost, but there are other ways. But like the original bonding, it takes time. I am convinced that because of all the complexities and dynamics involved with blending two families together it takes a minimum of at least two years before you can begin to become a single family unit. So don't give up. But it really does take time.

Start by not judging his or her kids by your own. Like you in your former relationship, your kids can be wrong. Sometimes the kids are just different, and not right or wrong. Usually this problem with the children comes to a head when you have to deal with disciplinary matters. Here again, the two of you need to sit down and talk. You need to develop a system you both agree on, and a system that can be applied *equally* to all of the children. Plan for surprises too! Realize that this is a different home, and a different set of rules. Be sure to discuss these new rules with the children. Don't start screaming at them as if they could read your mind about the new rules.

Another very important thing is that the children should not get away with treating the new mom or dad like some dog. Kids often have a way of realizing that the new parent is bending over backwards to make the new family situation work. As a result, they are quick to learn just how much they can get away with in terms of things they must or cannot do. This is not all that hard to work out, but what can be hard is the way your children treat your new mate when you are not around. They simply cannot be allowed to get away with treating your new husband or wife badly, and then hiding behind you. In one particular case, the husband let his older children talk to his new wife in a very disrespectful manner. And, if she said something about it the guy jumped on her and blamed her. Children do *not* talk to a mother or father (blood or step) in a disrespectful manner. I have always thought that children have a right to their feelings, but they don't have a right to treat a parent in a disrespectful manner. You simply cannot let the children treat your new partner in this manner. How would you like it if some child treated you in this manner? Cute it ain't! At the same time, *you* must also treat your new mate in a respectful manner. If you don't, look at the model you are setting for the children to follow. Remember, a relationship grows and continues when the parties are seen in each other's eyes as equal, and the individuals involved show a genuine respect for each other. This is not done by you or your children treating your new mate in a derogatory manner.

Yet another thing that you should do is spend some extra time with all of the children. There are times when you should spend time with just your children. This is fine as long as it is balanced by your spending time with his or her children, and, of course, all of the children together. The new children should not feel that you put up with them because they came along as a package deal with your new mate. If you reflect this, they will never have a chance to learn to love you. You and the new children must meet on some neutral or common ground and begin to share time. Talk, do things together, and give each other an honest chance to let your relationship grow. It can grow, but this is just one thing you can't rush.

Some of the new children feel that you are trying to take the place of their mom or dad who is no longer living with them. Don't insist on their calling you mom or dad. They will resent you for it. Remember, the children didn't ask for the original divorce and they didn't ask for the new relationship either. It is hard enough just growing up in our complex world without being thrust into a situation that you don't like and putting up with other kids in a new house or sharing what had only been your room and house with these "other kids." At any rate, making a blended family work is more work than making an original family work. I think that is why so many individuals end up in a second divorce. They weren't willing to put out the extra work to make the original family unit work, so how are they going to make a new family succeed that requires even more work? It can be done!

Growing out of the above point is also the idea that you shouldn't degrade each other's "exes." If you talk negatively about your ex-wife or ex-husband that puts a burden on the children who really love their other parent, even if you no longer do. If you continually use the approach of degrading the other parent, the children will, in time, isolate themselves emotionally from you and your new mate. Besides, it is not a good example to set for anybody. If you just don't talk about the other parent who is not there, you won't put yourself in a difficult position with your own or your new partner's children. No matter how you look at it, it is an approach that leads to a dead end. So, don't do it.

Another aspect growing out of this kind of behavior is the fact that each parent has a right to a relationship with his or her child. Sometimes as parents we really mess up that relationship, but it's a relationship that belongs to us. Don't attempt to make your husband or wife have a relationship with his or her child that is only under your terms. Your value judgments are no better than anyone else's, and in time, both your mate and the child will resent you for doing what you did to their relationship.

At the same time each child has a right to his or her relationship with each of his or her individual parents. A relationship with someone is very personal. Despite what others think of your relationship and what you do or don't do with it, it belongs to you. Hopefully, you will treat the relationships you have with dignity and care, but even if you don't, you have a right to your relationship with others as does your spouse and all of the children.

Yet another item that is often overlooked in the new blended family is the rate at which change is expected. Be it discipline, how or what they eat, how they act, or almost everything else that you can think of, the rate of change is going to be slow. When a child is born it takes the child a few years to become a part of and learn all of the dos and don'ts of a family. The same is true of the new blended family except that they not only have to learn all the new things, but they must also forget many of the old rules and habits. When you go too fast with the child, it can lead to frustration and unhappiness for all.

Also, when the children are learning the "right" things to do, they are going to make mistakes. When you are learning something new, don't you make mistakes? Sure you do. Don't forget they are just kids and they may make many mistakes with their learning. If you don't think children make mistakes, take a careful look at their schoolwork when they come home, or listen to them practice their musical instruments, especially a violin. Oh, do they make mistakes! They are also going to make mistakes in their adjustments. In your adjustment process make room for these mistakes, just as you make room in your life for your own mistakes.

This chapter does not change the various points that were made earlier in this book. The ways to interact with your mate, how to discipline and how to treat and train your children, still apply. But, other things need to be considered when you are dealing with your new marriage partner and children in the blended family. Although I have presented only a few points, I hope you can take the principles behind these points and apply them to your unique situation. Good luck, and remember it takes t-i-m-e.

Things to Remember

1. Talk to your mate and handle problems as they arise.
2. Make time and take that time for love in your life.
3. Spend time with *all* of the children.
4. Don't make the children call you mom or dad.
5. Don't say bad things about your ex-mates.
6. Adjustment takes time. Give the children and yourself enough time and allow for mistakes in the adjustment process.

12. How to Handle Stress

There is a thing in men, women, and children that is called stress. It has become the plague of modern mankind. Part of the problem is that we have a nervous system that still belongs in the wild. The other primary part of the problem is that we never really learn how to handle the problems that come our way in life. Mom or dad didn't show us how to accept or deal with the fact that our favorite toy was broken or we had to go visit grandma when we wanted to be with our friend or the problem we had with that bully at school or even the teacher we didn't like. Chances are that neither mom nor dad knew how to handle these things either. In school, from kindergarten all the way through high school, no one ever had a class on handling life. In fact, too many of the things we learn in school will probably make life more confusing and difficult. Remember Latin, algebra, or chemistry? So, where do we really learn how to cope with stress and the problems of life as they come along? Being raised, in part, by my grandparents, I used to think that knowledge about life came with age. I especially remember my grandmother who could turn almost any crisis into nothing at all. She could turn any storm into a calm sea. The problem in today's society is that most kids can't take advantage of an extended family and benefit from grandma's wisdom. Too often, not even mom or dad is around.

What to do? Well, I'd like to pretend I'm my own grandma (perhaps I need therapy) and give you a few points to think about in terms of handling stress. You can practice these things for your own life as well as teach these approaches to stress to your kids. Again, these won't answer every crisis you are ever going to have, but I think they will at least start you in the right direction. I call these points my "calming pills." Let's take a few of these pills and see what happens.

Calming pill 1. Take one thing at a time.

One of the difficulties that I have seen both children and adults have is that they don't seem to be able to handle one thing at a time. This applies to emotional issues that are bothering them, as well as problems that arise in the course of everyday life.

Let's take the emotional issues first. Often when things bother us, we don't say anything to anyone because we don't want to hurt their feelings, or we just simply don't know how to tell people that things have hurt our feelings. If someone hurts your feelings or makes you angry, you must say something to the person who is hurting you or making you angry. If you do not tell the person, how will he or she know that he or she is doing this to you? Although there are a few people that enjoy hurting other people's feelings, they are a small minority. So tell the person. The other individual can't read your mind. If you tell most people that they are hurting you or making you angry they will try to modify their behavior. Now, be sure to tell them in a way that doesn't anger them either. If you do, you are back where you started from.

If someone has hurt you, go to that person, in private, and tell the person in a nice way what he or she has done to hurt your feelings. If you do this the two of you can begin to work on those issues that are a problem to each of you. But do it early when the problems are very little ones. If you wait until the problems are gigantic, they can get out of hand and then almost everyone gets hurt and loses (e.g., a divorce). Do it patiently when things arise. Remember, just because you and your mate love each other, that doesn't mean that you can read each other's minds. You have to *work* at communicating, and you do that with practice. If the children see you talking to each other when "little problems" arise, and watch the two of you resolve difficulties, they will learn an appropriate pattern as they grow. You will still have an occasional disagreement, but this is normal and healthy. It certainly can clear the air. The kids can see that you can get angry and still be in love. Talking resolves difficulties, and it is fun to make up.

The other aspect of this has to deal with things that arise in plain ol' living. Maybe you received a speeding ticket today and you had to work overtime and you just don't feel good. If you have lived life at all, there are days that it seems that life itself is out to get you. This is when you can teach the children a valuable lesson as well as make life a lot more pleasant for yourself. Stop a minute before you start your list of things that bother you and take them one at a time. I'm sure you recall the tale of the straw that broke the camel's back. If we can train ourselves and our children to take things one at a time as they arise, we can teach them that even the most difficult things can be handled. I cannot lift a ton, but if I move a few pounds at a time, a few pounds that I can handle, I can move the ton easily. The same is true of our problems. We are creative problem-solving beings, but when we don't use those abilities, life can crush us under its weight.

Take things one at a time and use your creative talents to solve problems and put them in their place. Then forget it. Reward yourself and then go on to problem number two. What a lesson to teach your children! Do you want your children to copy your life problem-solving abilities or do you want them to learn how to solve problems in a constructive manner? Remember they are watching you.

Most psychologists will tell you that only a small fraction of the things that you worried about ever come true, nor will worrying be of any help. So stop it. Do something about your emotions or problems as they arise, before they grow out of control. Again, isn't this the lesson you want to teach your children?

Calming pill 2. Don't take your problems to bed.

Closely related to pill 1 is calming pill 2. In the process of handling the things as they come along I strongly recommend, from my own experience, that you do not take these problems to bed with you. This is certainly easier said than done and sometimes it is a very hard pill to swallow. On the back of my bedroom door I have a pretend hook. At night before I go to bed, I make it a policy to hang the problems of the day on that hook. I get a good night's sleep and I am refreshed for the next day, ready to start on the next day's or any other problem.

I'm not saying that using this hook is easy to learn or that it will work everytime. But, this has worked for me and if your children see that you are able to do this, and they get a chance to practice this adjustment mechanism, by the time they are adults they will be able to do it. I am a lot more pleasant, easier to live with, and I'm a lot better at solving a problem when I've had a good night's sleep. I'd be willing to bet that you are too. Give the "problem hook" a chance and see if it is a pill your system will accept.

Calming pill 3. Laugh at yourself.

Of all the pills I can give you, I think this is one of the most important ones. Some people get so involved in what they are doing that they think that unless "they" do it (whatever it is), it just won't get done right. These people are taking themselves too seriously, and they need to take a step back and laugh at themselves. Here is a real lesson to teach your children.

We learn in the journey through life that there are many people who can do what we do and many of them can even do it better. Don't think that you are so important that only "you" can do something, whatever it is, and that if it can't be done the world is just going to end. Relax, take a step back, and laugh at yourself. I often work on my car. If you have ever done this, you know that there are times when you want to take the wrench you are working with, or sometimes even the car, and throw it in the trash or in the empty field near your house. In fact, when I used to get angry at my car, when I couldn't fix what I wanted to fix, I used to take my wrench and give it a pitch. My oldest son now has the same habit (I can't imagine where he got it from).

Take the time to laugh at yourself and try to see how really funny we can be when we are doing something stupid. Besides, when you are laughing you are using the parasympathetic nervous system. That is the system associated with being relaxed. And, if you are relaxed, how can you get an ulcer or hypertension or feel a lot of stress? As before, what a lesson to teach your children!

Calming pill 4. Add variety.

There are times when we get very involved with things and there certainly isn't anything wrong with this to a point. But, overall, we need some variety. I love spaghetti, but I don't eat it three times a day. You should try to add variety to your life. Variety is a benefit to you now and will be of greater benefit as you grow older. I'm not saying that you shouldn't have some favorite things that you like to do, but I am saying that you should not limit yourself to just one thing in life. This probably isn't going to make a lot of sense at first, but you shouldn't just live your life for your mate, your parents, your kids, bowling, fishing, or whatever. Not just one thing. What happens if you lose this one thing? How are you going to survive psychologically? You can't just crawl into a corner and give up. If you have some variety in life and you lose one of your life supports, your ship of life won't go down.

A friend of mine lived just to play softball and he was quite good at it. While at work one day he had an accident. As a result, he can no longer play softball. He had an adjustment problem that you wouldn't believe. If he would have expanded his interests to include several things, he would have had an easier time during this difficult adjustment period. It would also have been easier on his wife and children. They really paid a heavy price psychologically.

Give yourself a chance to develop a number of life supports. This is why we have children trying a little of this and a little of that as they grow up. We are teaching them to enjoy a variety of life's games. If we take a lesson from them, we will find that this variety will keep us interested and excited about life and we won't be putting all of our psychological eggs in one basket.

Calming pill 5. Give love away.

Right up there with laughing at yourself, giving love away is a *very* important calming pill. What I mean by that is this: as you meet people in life be friendly, helping, and kind. What does it cost you? By giving love away we can help make a world we will want our children to live in.

We live in a world that grows smaller by the hour. As it rapidly grows smaller and smaller, we are becoming more crowded and are living with the kinds of diversity that our grandparents never dreamed of. In my small neighborhood live a mix of different races and nationalities that just a few years ago one would have had to travel the world over to meet. And the world is just going to keep getting smaller and smaller. Our parents and especially our grandparents would have had difficulty making today's living adjustments. We are traveling through space on a planet that has become only slightly larger than one house. We cannot afford the racial and religious prejudice that our ancestors bathed in. If we are ever to succeed in this venture called life, we must abandon these old ways of living and reach out the hand of love to all those with whom we come into contact. What a gift to leave to our children! To be able to love those around us who are different, different for whatever reason. We don't want a single race or belief; that would be very boring. But, to be able to love and respect the differences around us; now, there is a gift we can teach our children. As they see you doing this, they will share in the process. What too many, for too long, have done with their fears and prejudices has led to where? Nowhere.

If we can pass on the lesson of giving love away to those around us and those with whom we come into contact, think of the world we could build. We haven't done such a hot job thus far, what have we to lose? Are you big enough to teach this valuable lesson to your children?

Calming pill 6. Get some exercise.

After all of the psychological things we have talked about, you probably think that I'm off my rocker to talk about exercise. Actually, exercise can create a double effect if you are willing to participate. First, it can become one of several excellent mechanisms that have the potential of draining stress from our mind and its negative effects from our body. Second, it is physically good for you. You will actually feel better physically and psychologically.

Now, you don't have to look like Arnold Schwartzennegger or Victoria Principal. What am I talking about is making some type of exercise a part of your life's diet. Some people like tennis, some jogging, some swimming, or there are a host of things that you can do to get some exercise. Research clearly indicates that it is good for your health and if you do get sick, you will recover quicker if you are in good shape. Of course, if you haven't been exercising with any regularity, you need to consult your doctor to see if you are able to exercise and to determine if there are any restrictions that the doctor will place on you. If you can do some type of exercise, start sensibly. If you don't, it may hurt you or make you so sore that you will not want to exercise. Start with small amounts and gradually build the time and level of physical output involved. Remember, you want to get and stay healthy, not kill yourself. Also, get the whole family in on it. They may not like to do what you do, but encourage them to *do something*. If kids just sit and watch television and play Nintendo, they are not getting exercise they need. Exercising is a hard thing to start if it has not been a part of your life, but if you will get into it you will not believe the difference it will make in your physical and psychological health.

Calming pill 7. Try God.

Finally, the last topic in the book. I certainly do not want to convert you to some religion and I'm certainly no crusader. But each of you, in your own way, ought to make God a part of your life. I have tried to lay before you all of the things that I have learned and experienced that have helped me raise my kids as well as make my life more meaningful. My belief in God is a very important part of my life and when all else has failed me, He has not. Why not give it a try? It has worked for me and this too is an excellent lesson to pass on to your children. Take it a little at a time, but give it a try. It is a gift to your children that will last an eternity.

Things to Remember

1. Take one thing at a time.
2. Don't take your problems to bed.
3. Laugh at yourself.
4. Add variety.
5. Give love away.
6. Get some exercise.
7. Try God.